Routledge Revivals

A Short History of Harmony

A Short History of Harmony

Charles Macpherson

Routledge
Taylor & Francis Group

First published by Kegan Paul, Trench, Trübner & Co. Ltd

This edition first published in 2018 by Routledge
2 Park Square, Milton Park, Abingdon, Oxon, OX14 4RN
and by Routledge
711 Third Avenue, New York, NY 10017

Routledge is an imprint of the Taylor & Francis Group, an informa business

Publisher's Note
The publisher has gone to great lengths to ensure the quality of this reprint but points out that some imperfections in the original copies may be apparent.

Disclaimer
The publisher has made every effort to trace copyright holders and welcomes correspondence from those they have been unable to contact.

A Library of Congress record exists under ISBN: unk84131446

ISBN 13: 978-1-138-60263-2 (hbk)
ISBN 13: 978-1-138-60268-7 (pbk)
ISBN 13: 978-0-429-45711-1 (ebk)

A SHORT HISTORY OF HARMONY

BY

CHARLES MACPHERSON

ORGANIST OF ST PAUL'S CATHEDRAL, PROFESSOR OF HARMONY AT THE ROYAL ACADEMY OF MUSIC, FELLOW OF THE ROYAL ACADEMY OF MUSIC, FELLOW OF THE ROYAL COLLEGE OF ORGANISTS

WITH NUMEROUS MUSICAL ILLUSTRATIONS

THIRD IMPRESSION

LONDON

KEGAN PAUL, TRENCH, TRUBNER & CO., LTD.

BROADWAY HOUSE, 68–74 CARTER LANE, E.C.

TO

STEWART MACPHERSON

AND

JOHN B. McEWEN

FELLOW-PROFESSORS

AT THE ROYAL ACADEMY OF MUSIC

AS AN ACKNOWLEDGMENT OF INDEBTEDNESS

TO THEIR

TEXT-BOOKS ON HARMONY

THIS LITTLE BOOK

IS

GRATEFULLY INSCRIBED

PREFACE

Written primarily for the use of those to whom music is essentially a pastime, it is hoped that this little work—though far from claiming to be a text-book—may be of some service, even to others who have adopted music as a serious study.

It has been the author's aim to write in a style midway between the bare statement of facts on the one hand and over-elaboration of detail on the other. The indulgence of the reader is craved if this aim has not been achieved.

Special (and perhaps at first sight undue) attention has been given to the earlier phases of harmony, for it is the writer's opinion that the ability to appreciate the later developments of harmony rests largely upon a proper understanding of what has happened in former times.

The reader is earnestly advised to play over all the examples that he cannot "hear" in his mind.

CONTENTS

DEFINITIONS

THE following definitions of a few words that will be frequently met with may be found useful in preventing confusion.

Chord.—A simultaneous combination of notes. A chord is either concordant or dissonant, i.e. either a concord or a discord. The latter contains one or more dissonant notes; a concord contains no dissonant note.

Progression.—Two different chords sounded in succession form a progression.

Harmonic.—(1) Adjective formed from the word "harmony."

(2) Noun—a note of faint quality produced by some aliquot part of a vibrating musical medium. The whole substance of this medium produces the real or foundation note (p. 13).

(The context will be sufficient guide to show which of these two meanings is intended.)

Chromatic.—(1) Notes foreign to the scale or key; e.g. F sharp is *chromatic* in the scale or key of C.

(2) Music containing such notes is said to be chromatic. Modulation (p. 8) is not induced by chromatic notes.

Diatonic.—(1) Notes belonging to the scale or key; e.g. F sharp is *diatonic* in the key of G, as it belongs to the scale.

(2) Music consisting entirely of such notes is said to be diatonic.

A SHORT HISTORY OF HARMONY

CHAPTER I

INTRODUCTORY

HARMONY, the art of combining musical sounds, occupies a large share of attention at the present day. Its practice has become so varied and widened, that certain composers have gone so far as to evolve systems of their own on which to build their compositions. This fact, together with the great development of harmony on more normal lines, has of course had its reflection in the public attitude towards music generally.

People begin to recognise pieces by this or that series of 'beautiful chords,'—some of which would have caused their grandfathers great mental pain—they no longer display the same frenzied satisfaction, punctuated by nodding of heads and the exchange of knowing smiles, when anything resembling a melody is discovered, regardless of how bald and ridiculous the accompaniment may be. Few people possessed of an educated ear any longer listen only to the top part or melody, or only to the most prominent part in whatever voice or instrument it may appear. The harmonic structure together with the general texture of a piece of music now also make their appeal to the cultivated listener ; it is more than likely, too, that were some melodies or subjects re-harmonised, i.e. founded on a different harmonic basis, they would fail to be recognised. In short, harmony has become one of the factors that help to regulate popular interest in music.

If the following example were played over, many would fail to recognise it as a re-harmonisation and transposition[1] of a well-known and oft-quoted subject.

Ex. I

Of course this is a shocking travesty from a harmonic and many other points of view ;

[1] i.e. put into another key.

for it treats the upper part of the original as a continuous melody, thus destroying the real trend of the parts or voices. Also, instead of allowing the first three notes to tell their own tale without any accompaniment, our present example must needs provide two other parts, which are about as useful as people who stand gazing at a street accident without doing anything to help. In the original too, the climax is reached at the point A, and not until then is the aid of harmony called in with the twofold object of re-inforcing the sound and providing just the right chord for the desired expressive effect. It is unnecessary to enlarge on the further enormities of this example. Its glaring inanities and inexpressiveness will at once be apparent when compared with the original, in Ex. 64.

When composers began to write in a style which included many harmonic novelties, together with a more complicated style of accompaniment, they placed themselves at once outside the pale of general popularity. Before Wagner's time, for instance, the type of music which held popular sway was of a less intricate nature. The arias of Italian Operas to a large extent constituted the musical food of the general public. In these there was little or no compelling interest beyond the melody itself.

Listeners therefore were not greatly concerned with the accompaniment, still less so with the general structure of the music.

Though great composers had already written immortal works, they were not known. Bach was practically a sealed book to all but a select few; Mozart and Beethoven were not appreciated as they are now,—audiences sometimes talked all through a Beethoven Symphony — and when smaller composers strove to imitate them, it was nearly always the melodic side only of their model that they chose as their pattern. The results obtained by these means were like—

> 'Little Tom Noddy,
> All head and no body.'

At the present day we have curious instances of the converse of all this. Composers who have attained distinction in their treatment of harmony usually have numberless imitators who do not possess the insight to appreciate the poetic promptings of the true artist. The outcome is a mass of compositions of a heterogeneous description—mere musical scrap-books of harmonic abnormalities, strung together without any central idea of purpose or design

Though harmony plays such an important part in music, it is but one aspect of the art. It influences most other musical considerations, and in turn is itself much modified by them. Let us briefly examine a few of these considerations.

Melody

Melody is one of the prime factors in determining the choice of chords. Harmony must be used which will fit the tune. Though this is an accepted and obvious fact, yet there are some works in which the converse seems to hold good—the melody has been manufactured to accommodate some preconceived harmonic idea.

Accent

A great deal of the effect of a chord is dependent upon the position it occupies in a bar of music. If a chord falls on an accent the effect is not the same as when it falls on a weak portion of the bar. By altering the accentuation of a tune, we can make it sound quite absurd, even though we retain every chord of the original. If we play *Home Sweet Home* thus :

Ex. 2

it becomes quite out of gear, as the accents fall in the wrong places. We must, however, take into consideration the fact, that there are some people with so little sense of rhythm or accent that they would notice no difference in this perverted version of the tune.

Rhythm

Rhythm is of course closely allied with accent. The Time spent upon any one chord has a determining influence upon its value or

Rhythmic alteration of *God Save the King.*

Ex. 3

effect. By altering the rhythm of a tune while retaining the original harmony, we can distort it still further, even sufficiently to make it unrecognisable by the entirely unmusical. For the entirely unmusical, more often than not, refuse to fall into nets spread for them by their more musical friends.

Environment and Tonality

The question of general environment is one of great importance in regulating the effect of any chord or succession of chords. If we play the following example as far as the double bar-line, then, after a short pause, play the chord following, the latter has quite a startling effect, though it is but the very common chord of C major.

Ex. 4

The reason for this is that there is no note in the common chord of C major which occurs in the key of F sharp major—the key in which the example begins. This concerns tonality.

Tonality implies the existence of some note which we feel to be the central point of rest. In straightforward music it is not usually difficult for the ear to fix on this note, which is called the *tonic* or *key-note.* As long as this note remains the centre round which the harmony revolves, the music is said to remain in the key of that note. When the harmony gravitates towards another central note, the mind rejects the former key-note as the centre of rest, and we arrive in a new key. This process is termed modulation, and every chord that was used with reference to the former key-note bears an entirely fresh relationship to it as soon as the new key-note has been established.

When we hear of a new chord being discovered by someone, it is very often nothing more than a well-known combination of sound used in connection with an unusual key-note.

One chord by itself is not sufficient to tell us in what key a piece of music is written ; we must hear something before or after it, to show us exactly what is meant in the way of tonality or key.

It we were to listen to the first chord of Mendelssohn's *Wedding March* it would mean nothing; but if we continued we should certainly know our bearings on reaching the point marked *, if not sooner.[1]

MENDELSSOHN'S *Wedding March.*

Ex. 5

[1] Though the first chord of the March makes an excursion to E minor the fact is fortuitous and the chord belongs to C major. In fact it is possible to go straight from this chord to the point marked *.

We can say the same of the following extract from Rachmaninoff's Prelude in C sharp minor. The marked chord is quite indefinite in character, and it is only when we play what follows that we appreciate its tonality value.

Prelude in C sharp minor (RACHMANINOFF)

Ex. 6

It is interesting to observe, that on a keyed instrument the two chords under notice are identical, excepting that in the case of the Prelude another note of the combination stands at the top, a fact which does not alter the nature of the chord any more than does the mere reduplication of notes.

It should be stated, too, that notes forming chords are always reckoned from the bass, i.e. the lowest note sounded, or understood as still holding good. In the Mendelssohn example, for instance, A is the bass note of the first chord; A is also the bass note in the Rachmaninoff extract at the marked point, as it still holds good.

We have said that it does not matter how many times a note is reduplicated—*doubled* is the easier and technical term—in a chord. Neither does it matter in what order the notes stand above a bass note.

With regard to the two examples just given, we repeat that one chord by itself cannot define a key. In this particular case we have seen that the same chord (i.e. the same as far as the ear is concerned, excepting the little unessential difference already noted) can be used in two keys so distantly related. It is only when we appreciate the value of this chord with reference to each key-note that its chameleon-like properties are apparent.

It is clear then that a chord by itself is of no value whatever. We must have a progression of two or more chords before we are aware of any key-note or tonal centre.

There are numerous minor considerations between which and harmony there is some mutual influence.

Duration

The length of time for which a chord is sounded in comparison with its neighbours is significant in determining its effect. This obvious fact can be proved by playing over Ex. 3, where by reason of the rhythmic disturbance the chords acquire a different value.

Pitch

A chord is affected by pitch, i.e. the height or depth at which it is played. Take a few simple chords, such as are in Ex. 4, and play them as they stand. Then play them an octave or two higher, then lower. The effect is not by any means the same. It is analogous to looking at a photograph successively through differently coloured glasses.

Quantity and Quality of Sound

The quantity and quality of sound employed to produce a chord are factors not to be disregarded.

A chord played very loudly does not sound exactly the same as when it is played very softly. The mass of sound has some bearing upon the effect.

So, too, the nature of the medium employed has a qualifying tendency. A chord played by four violins does not sound the same as when it is played by four flutes or four trumpets. This phenomenon, however, is largely due to another reason. Every note that is sounded contains the 'ghosts' of several other higher notes, called *harmonics*.[1] It is the varying predominance of these harmonics that constitutes the difference in *timbre* or quality of sound, and in a secondary way modifies the effect of harmony.

It would be quite possible to extend the list of minor details which have some influence upon the effect of harmony. We will mention only one other—resonance.

The late Sir John Stainer used to say that even a sneeze sounded magnificent in St. Paul's Cathedral. It remains true that some music which in that highly resonant building sounds dignified and effective, would not sound so well in a building of no resonance. There is music too which does not 'come off' where there is much echo in a building.

To sum up: we have seen that harmony, though of the highest importance, is not every-

[1] The following represents some of the 'harmonics' thrown off by the lowest note C. If this note is struck and sustained on a good piano, it is possible to hear the upper notes appearing in turn.

thing in music. It is subject to many other considerations, some of which have been enumerated.

The earliest and most important constructive influence upon the development of harmony was counterpoint. We shall reserve a discussion of this matter to a later chapter.

CHAPTER II

BIRTH OF HARMONY

WITH regard to harmony, as indeed with most other branches of music, practice has usually outstripped theory. Textbooks on harmony nowadays enunciate modifications of what were once hard-and-fast rules, in order to accord with the latest developments of composers who have said something, perhaps old, in a new way.

"Art is free," said old Haydn, and as to rules he added, "the educated ear is the sole authority on all these questions, and I think I have as much right to lay down the law as anyone."

This statement does not mean that theory is in any way to be neglected or lightly treated. The fully-equipped musician who has not had to submit to its irksomeness has yet to be discovered. A close study of theory is of course indispensable to the earnest student.

The 'laying down the law' mentioned by Haydn is quite permissible to those possessed of the requisite 'educated ear,' but at the hands of those not so qualified the act becomes nothing short of a veritable curse in musical matters.

The ancient Greeks possessed a highly organised system of theory, but so rigid, that it was no more capable of extension than the Standard Yard measure at Greenwich Observatory. One writer has ventured to assert that progress in music only became possible in proportion as the Greek system decayed. Though the Greeks knew the nature of musical intervals, i.e. the distance between any two notes, it is now generally believed that they never made use of any harmony. Their music was therefore entirely melodic, perhaps sung in unison or octaves.

There seems to be little doubt that the Greek system of scales was drawn upon by Bishop Ambrose of Milan in the fourth century, and again in the sixth century by Pope Gregory. These two great men helped to establish the modes or scales on some recognised footing.

Scales are of course of vital importance to harmony, and it is impossible to imagine what would have been the trend of harmony, had not musicians been eventually forced, after long and tedious experiment, to accept the modern major scale—in place of the ancient modes—as the basis of further operations.

We have not space to describe fully the ancient modes or scales. It must suffice to say that they may be represented on the piano by starting a scale on any note of the scale of C major, and continuing upwards for an octave without using any black note. The difference in effect between the scales or modes will be apparent. This is caused by the semitones (E to F and B to C) falling between different degrees of the scale in each mode.

In using these ancient modes, singers employed an occasional B flat or F sharp to correct the augmented fourth, or *tritone*, existing between F and B, wherever this *diabolus in musicâ* stood out too prominently. This was originally for melodic reasons only, for as may be inferred from what has been said, melody was invented centuries before harmony.

We have stated that the Greeks knew the nature of intervals. But, as they rejected as discords all intervals except the fourth, fifth and octave, with their compounds,[1] it is not difficult to see why they never attempted anything in the way of harmony.

What went on in the way of actual musical performance between the Greek era and the tenth century is more or less a matter of conjecture, and we do not know the date when the first daring experiment of performing two

[1] A compound is an interval greater than an octave, *e.g.* a compound fourth is a fourth *plus* an octave.

notes simultaneously was made. But we have a shrewd suspicion as to how this came about.

Taking the four greater divisions of human voices, a glance at the following will show that each class of voice has an upper limit of about a fifth above the next class.

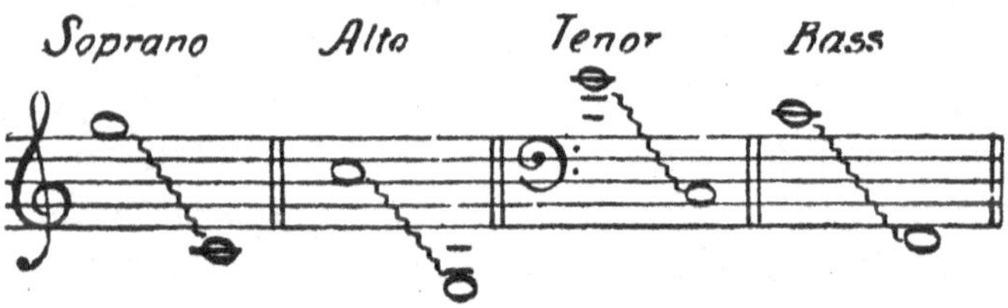

Ex. 7

Notice too, that the tenor and bass compasses are at the distance of an octave below the soprano and alto respectively.

The early Christians perhaps started, very naturally, to sing their music in unison, any women present singing the same melody an octave higher.

If the music happened to be of a large compass, the upper notes in the course of repetition would tend to become trying for the lower classes of men's voices. Similarly, high voices would in process of time tire of the recurring low notes.

To obviate this physical difficulty, we can imagine experiments being made by the male portion of the congregation, of singing in an interval which is of all the most perfect, viz. the octave. Here again, a very little of this kind of singing would tax the vocal resources of tenors and basses, for their respective compasses are ranged at about a fifth apart. Hence the greater distance of an octave would in time produce a great strain on the singers.

Thus it came about that intervals were chosen which were more in accord with the natural difference in vocal compass; and further, these intervals were to all intents and purposes the same as those which the Greeks called concords. These were the intervals of the fourth and fifth. The remaining Greek con-

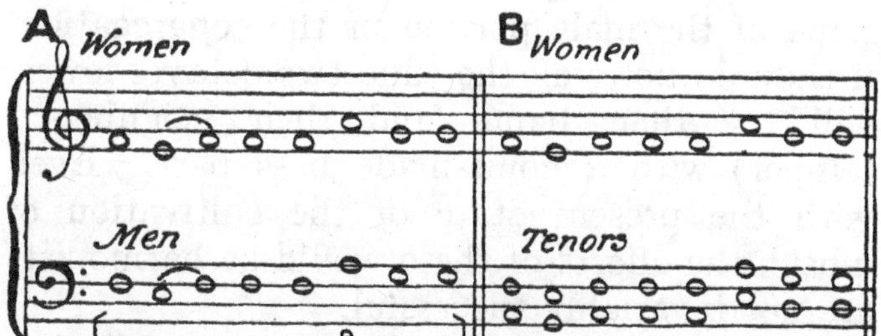

Ex. 8

cord, the octave, had already been tried, possibly with disastrous results to throats and voices.

Ex. 8 is a suggestion as to how the final result (Ex. 9) may have been evolved. A shows the men and women singing in unison, the women performing their part an octave above the men. The basses finding the recurring upper notes too trying, and the bracketed small notes ineffective and equally tiring, chose a half-way-house note, as shown in B. A corresponding state of things in the women's voices gives us the combined result in Ex. 9, as we shall see presently.

There is a common experience, even now, when such a thing as an unaccompanied hymn-tune is sung in unison by many voices. After a few verses it is more than likely that some of the ladies will try to 'put in a second,' while some of the male portion of the congregation if they do not sing the tune two octaves lower will try their hand (and their neighbour's temper) with a home-made bass part. Even with the present state of the cultivation of music, the efforts of these would-be harmonists are not invariably successful.

It is important to observe that this improvised harmonising is not always due to the desire of procuring artistic effect, but rather is it an attempt to discover some comfortable compass in which the vocal efforts of the singer may gyrate.

The system of singing in fourths and fifths and octaves is described by Hucbald, a monk of St. Amand in Flanders, who died at an advanced age A.D. 930.

Though he wrote a learned treatise *Musica Enchiriadis*, it is quite open to question whether he really invented the systems he describes. It is perfectly possible that he attempted to give an account of music as he found it, rather than set himself up as a discoverer.

The name *organum* was given by Hucbald to this system of singing in fourths and fifths. " From this mingling of sounds you will see is born a sweet harmony,"[1] said he. Here is a short specimen of the ' sweet harmony ' :

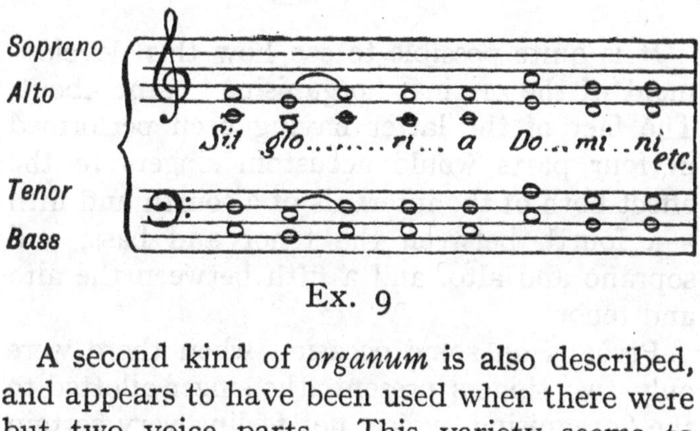

Ex. 9

A second kind of *organum* is also described, and appears to have been used when there were but two voice parts. This variety seems to

[1] " Videbis nasci sauvem ex hâc sonorum commixtione concentum."

have been based on the principle of each voice beginning on the same note. The principal voice sang the plainsong, while the ' organising ' voice either remained on its original note, thus forming what is termed a pedal, or sang in fourths or fifths, or in unison with the theme, as necessity or choice dictated.

Ex. 10

It is quite possible to see how this development of the original ' organising ' came about. The fact of the latter having been performed in four parts would accustom singers to the effect both of the intervals of a fourth and fifth —a fourth between the tenor and bass, and soprano and alto, and a fifth between the alto and tenor.

Perhaps on some occasion when there were only two singers present, the singer allotted to the ' organising ' voice, not feeling very certain of his intervals, elected to start on the same note as the ' principalis,' allowing the latter to sing on till the required interval came along, while he himself remained singing on one note until such time perhaps as his colleague should give him a friendly nudge as a hint to begin moving.

This is pure surmise, and it would not serve our purpose to suggest any further causes of the development. These may present themselves to the reader.

Though we may possibly smile at these early efforts, they cannot be regarded otherwise than in the light of being the birth of harmony. Indeed we may go further and say that if the first species (Ex. 9), however rude, was the forerunner of harmony, the second species (Ex. 10), as we shall see presently, anticipated counterpoint, inasmuch as it involved the use of 'passing-notes' (p. 32).

Be that as it may, singers were now becoming quite accustomed to the sound of more than one note simultaneously.

It can be imagined that the perpetually same treatment of themes would eventually suggest the desirability of novelty. And novelty was tried with a vengeance. Two or more tunes were chosen and performed simultaneously regardless of the effect. This was called *discant.* We know little of it beyond the fact that its employment must naturally have made musicians consider afresh the whole question of intervals, for there is a great difference between treating a theme on the one hand upon some recognised plan, and, on the other, trying to perform another melody against it, whether the two tunes fitted together or not. We can almost imagine the divided musical camps of those days. The adventurous practitioners of discant would hold cheap those who could not understand anything musical beyond organising, whilst those who clung to the organising tradition would stand aghast at the audacity of the 'new music.' For all that, the varied and independent movement of the parts in discant was a potent factor in the development of counterpoint. There was a gradual recognition of what really sounded well.

Franco of Cologne, possibly about the end of the twelfth century, gave many rules regarding discant. It certainly needed them, for it is one of the wildest practices in the history of music; and it is quite terrifying to think that this art was sometimes perpetrated in as many as five parts. Fortunately there are no examples in existence, for the examples of so-called discant are nothing more or less than counterpoint.

Franco seems to have been an innovator, for he condemned the old organising, and recommended the use both of perfect and imperfect concords. A curious point of his classification is that he reckoned both major and minor thirds as imperfect concords, while he described as imperfect *discords* the major and minor sixths.

It is an interesting fact that about this time (*c.* 1226), according to the late Mr. Rockstro, the English composition *Sumer is icumen in* appeared. This remarkable work, forming an epoch in musical history, and remaining as a wonder for all time, may be seen *in extenso* in *Grove's Dictionary* under its own title; and in the article on 'Schools of Composition' there is a facsimile of the Reading MS. of the work.

It is more than probable that the composition was the result of a series of happy accidents. Someone may have discovered that the tune could be sung by another voice starting four bars later, also that the process could be repeated until at length a *canon* for four voices was the result. Then to give more body to the sound, the two bass parts were possibly added last.

It must be remembered in these days when we can buy a miniature copy of *The Messiah* for sixpence, that the art of writing down music is the result of the labours of centuries. The mystery of placing musical thoughts upon paper was for a long period confined to men of the highest learning only. Thus we find that most of the early sources of information are connected with monasteries and other ecclesiastical institutions.

To return to Franco. Although he had condemned 'organising,' systems die hard, and there will always be found those to whom convention is the breath of life.

Whether Adam de la Hale was such a one we cannot say, for he lived before the days of trains, telegrams, and cheap postage, and possibly knew nothing of Franco's ideas. In the following example the old system of organising is still used as a background, but in detail there are a few interesting innovations in the way of embellishment. For all that, it is a futile production compared with the wondrous *Sumer is icumen in.*

ADAM DE LA HALE (*c.* 1280).

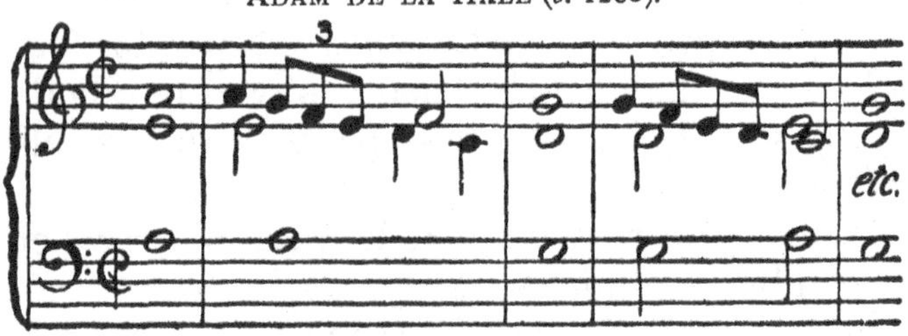

Ex. 11

We have now seen that the birth of harmony was more than likely due to the fact that singers of different ranges of voice found it physically impossible to perform melodic music either in unison or at the distance of an octave for any length of time. Hence, eventually they chose intervals which were more in requirement with the natural differences of vocal compass, and from this grew up the different kinds of organising, a system which, though rude in itself, was the forerunner of all further experiments in intervals.

The desire for novelty led people to invent discant, or the simultaneous performance of two or more tunes.

The outstanding drawback to all musical progress in these early times was the great difficulty experienced in writing down what composers wished; there was the further difficulty too of teaching singers to decipher the music when it had been written.

CHAPTER III

THE ALLIANCE OF HARMONY AND COUNTERPOINT

THE history of harmony is so bound up with that of counterpoint, that a brief definition of each will not be out of place.

Harmony concerns itself chiefly with the combining of musical sounds. Counterpoint is generally described as the art of combining melodies. Harmony takes a vertical, counterpoint a horizontal, view of music.

Though the derivation of the word counterpoint means 'note against note' (*punctum contra punctum*), the actual practice of counterpoint more often implies the art of writing more than one note against another. In other words, harmony pure and simple is written in notes of the same value or length in each voice, whereas the chief characteristic of counterpoint is a diversity and independence of movement between the parts, caused by the use of notes varying in length and pitch. An example will make this clearer :

Simple Two-part Harmony

The same subject treated in simple Two-part Counterpoint

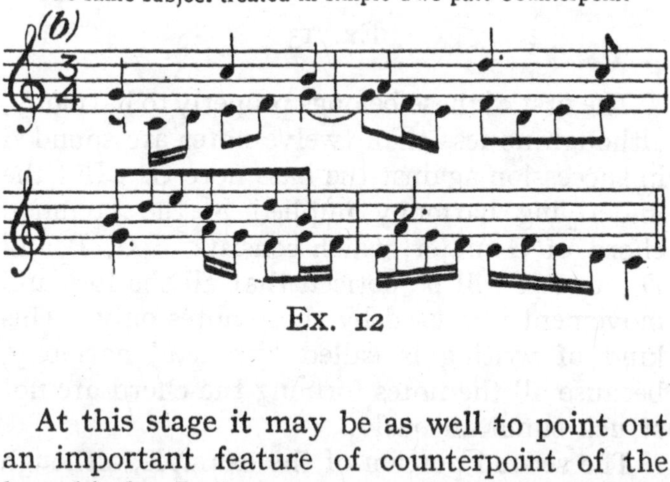

Ex. 12

At this stage it may be as well to point out an important feature of counterpoint of the best kind. In harmony proper of the simpler kind, every note that is struck belongs to the chord. In counterpoint a very large number of the notes do not belong to the harmony, but are used, for instance, to fill in the gaps, and for many other purposes. Compare the following:

Ex. 13

The first of these belongs properly to harmony, although no less than twelve notes are sounded in succession against the bass note G. But the underlying harmony implied is the common chord of G major, which consists of G, B and D; and it will be noticed that all the fuss and movement is caused by those notes only. This kind of writing is called 'broken' harmony, because all the notes forming the chord are not struck simultaneously.

The second portion of the example, although written on the same harmonic basis, contains notes outside the chord implied. These auxiliary, and passing, notes (*vide*. p. 33, Ex. 15, *et. seq*.) transform the first and simpler example into a mild contrapuntal effort.

The broken-harmony device is much used in piano music and the like ; while contrapuntal treatment is usually reserved for cases where the individual parts or voices demand some special significance or character.

Both harmony and counterpoint in theory and in practice have so much in common that it is sometimes difficult to draw a hard-and-fast line of demarcation. For the vertical consideration of counterpoint at any given moment of its progress has some definite reference to an implied harmonic basis ; and the horizontal aspect of all good harmonic part-writing should present a certain amount of the melodic curves demanded in counterpoint. In point of fact, paradoxical though it may sound, good harmonic part-writing is seldom obtained without the study of counterpoint ; and modern counterpoint cannot be written without a knowledge of harmony.

It is possible to have a piece of music written in a contrapuntal manner, yet consisting entirely of simultaneously struck chords —*punctum-contra-punctum,* or note against note—but in this case the music would only justify its title to counterpoint were each voice part written in some sort of melodic curve. Continual repetition of notes in any or all of the voices would destroy the curve, and the music would cease to be counterpoint.

Counterpoint always demands this melodic interest in all the voices or parts, and it is immaterial whether the interest is obtained by note-against-note writing, or by the blending of varied rhythms. The latter, however, is the higher type of counterpoint, and not only is it the medium by which all the greatest composers have attained their polyphonic[1] effects, but it is now regarded as the truer and almost exclusive definition of counterpoint.

In the case of harmony, any student who works intelligently through a modern treatise on the subject, will incidentally learn a very great deal about the practice of counterpoint; for in later treatises much more prominence has been given to details which belong, strictly speaking, more to the province of counterpoint than of harmony.

For instance, by the use of 'passing-notes,' or notes which fill in the gaps between harmony notes, the following innocuous specimen—

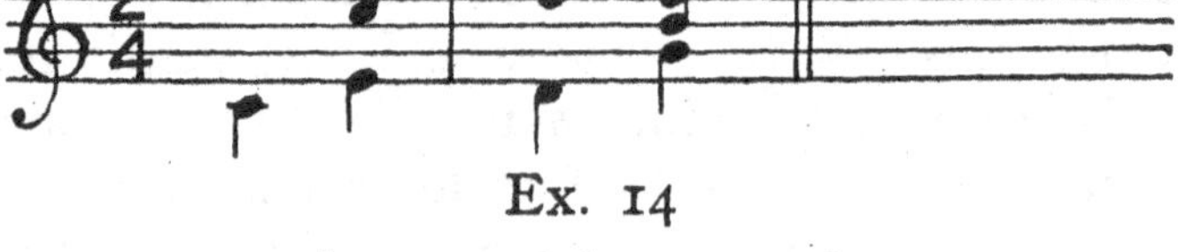

Ex. 14

[1] = many voices, or sounds.

could be somewhat enlivened into—

The notes marked + are passing-notes.

Ex. 15

Still further life and movement could be imparted by the addition of 'auxiliary notes,' or notes which lie immediately above and below each harmony note, to which they return. Thus we could evolve quite a little tune out of our dull and staid original.

The notes marked + are auxiliary notes.

Ex. 16

From this little example we can see what may be accomplished in harmony by the use of 'embroidery.' The result, obtained entirely by the devices acquired from the study of any modern treatise on harmony, has brought us into the realm of counterpoint. But when counterpoint is produced entirely by such embroidery, the underlying harmonic basis is much more easily discovered than in those cases where the music has been deliberately planned on some contrapuntal scheme. A simple example will help to show the increased difficulty of 'fixing' the harmony, when the underlying harmonic basis is almost overshadowed by the contrapuntal practice of allowing the parts to 'gang their ain gait.' The example is taken from Fugue No. 15 of J. S.

The notes of implied harmony are marked +.

Ex. 17

Bach's famous 48. Though, as we shall see later on, Bach's counterpoint was the result of a preconceived harmonic plan, the great composer had such a mighty grip of counterpoint that at times he almost obscured the harmonic scheme on which he was working.

Though the implied harmony here is perfectly plain—the first bar being a chord of the eventh on D, and the second bar a like chord formed from G,—the example is enough to show how the employment of this kind of counterpoint enhances the difficulty of analysing such music from the point of view of harmony. This difficulty is increased when more voices or parts are employed, and a simple example has been chosen purposely in order to exemplify a difficulty.

If we examine Ex. 17 more closely, we shall find one or two other interesting features. At first sight it looks as though it might be a piece of harmony as it is written in synchronising notes, i.e. notes sounded together. But it is not so, for many of the vertical combinations produce momentary discords—e.g. the second note in each hand, to name one instance only.

So it is not a case of the lower part trying to accommodate itself with the upper part note by note. And for the same reason it is not what is meant by note-against-note counterpoint. But the whole passage is an instance where a similar species of counterpoint is used in each part, each voice elaborating the implied chord on its own plan, and meeting in vertical or harmonic consonance at the principal accents of each bar as marked in the example.

From this example, and from almost any piece of good counterpoint, we can see that it is possible to discover vertical combinations of sound, which would never have been invented except by the use of counterpoint. These combinations are more the result of the varied rhythms or impelling individual melodic impetus of each voice than the regard to any supposed vertical requirements.

Such underlying vertical consideration does, however, exist, but it is subordinate to the melodic or horizontal requirements; and it is the study and practice of counterpoint which enable composers to determine for themselves how far the vertical aspect of music may be overruled by the horizontal.

Having now considered some of the features which are met with both in harmony and counterpoint, let us by way of antithesis draw attention to one particular detail, in which the two practices seem to differ considerably.

Take any good piece of counterpoint—a Bach fugue for instance—and it will be found quite easy to trace the progress of each voice in the composition.

J. S. BACH, Fugue No. 22 of the 48.

Ex. 18

The concluding chords of the first movement of Beethoven's Sonata in C minor, Op. 13, afford a good instance of harmonic progression pure and simple.

Here the music moves in masses of sound, and not, as in Ex. 18, according to the trend of each individual voice part. This is particularly apparent at the two bars marked *a*. The principle here involved is one that has reached a high state of development in later writers, and has been applied to chords much more distantly related than the two simple chords of our example. Modern instrumental writers frequently use certain chords as units for a par-

Ex. 19

ticular effect, and the relationship between them and the context is often hard to trace.

Harmony employed in this way may be said to have made an apparent break with counterpoint. For while counterpoint demands a logical sequence for each part, this pianistic harmonic writing aims at producing relays of sound, satisfactory in themselves but not necessarily strict as to the progression of the individual notes forming each chord.

In spite of this and other differences—the discussion of which space forbids—we have seen enough to convince us of the intimate connection between harmony and counterpoint.

We can only hope that, from the ore of these few general statements, the reader will be enabled to extract a little of the gold of truth.

CHAPTER IV

EARLY TECHNICAL PRACTICE

WE have seen how harmony began in a small way with the two forms of 'organising,' which were succeeded by discant, or the simultaneous performance of different tunes. All these methods helped to settle the question of intervals, and in process of time there was a survival of the fittest.

About the fourteenth century singers began to supply *faux-bourdons* to plainsong, one singer sustaining the theme, while others supplied the 'false '[1] parts at the intervals of a fourth and sixth below. The following is a portion of a fifteenth century *faux-bourdon.*

The top part is the subject, or *canto firmo.*

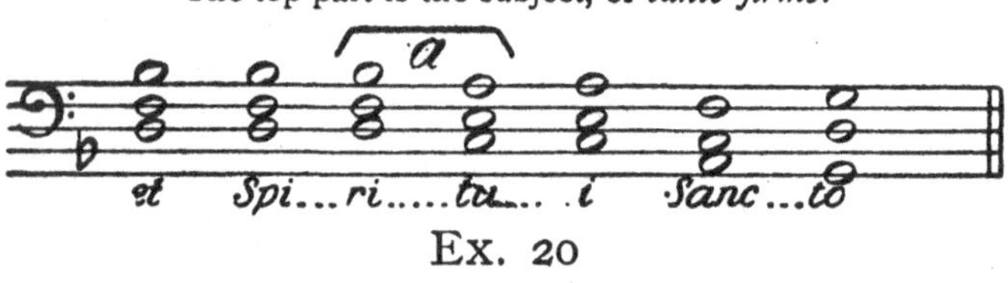

Ex. 20

[1] It has been suggested that the term 'false' was given to these extra parts in order to distinguish them from the old organising methods.

Both in the original organising, and in *faux-bourdons,* we find the same process of thought. As soon as a combination of sound was discovered which was satisfactory as an unit, each succeeding unit was treated on the same plan.

It is possible to suppose that, in the primitive state of music, singers would make occasional alterations either intentionally or otherwise. Such a thing as the following :

Ex. 21

(which together with the next two examples are variations of the portion marked *a* in Ex. 20) may have been an error originally, though now it is properly regarded as a legitimate effect, viz. a *suspension.* This means, that instead of all the voices moving together, as in Ex. 20, one voice holds its note until the others have moved.

The principle being established, it is not difficult to account for the following, now known as a *double suspension,* because the process is carried out by two voices.

Ex. 22

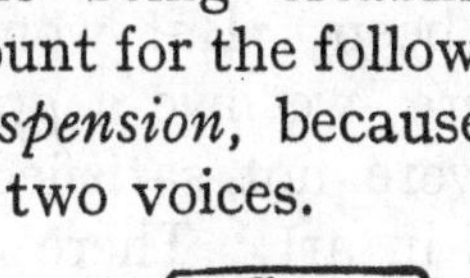

It is possible also that anticipatory notes—*anticipations*—were invented by accident, by means of one voice moving before the others. Thus we obtain the following variation :

Ex. 23

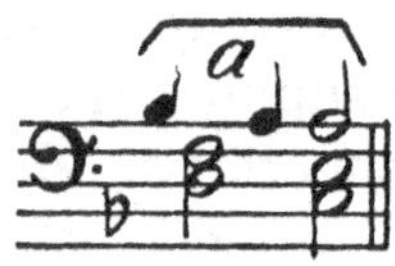

Throughout the history of music we find how large a share is played by ornamentation and elaboration. There have been in every age of musical art those whose insight seemed to carry their imagination far beyond the ken of their contemporaries. No one who is perfectly satisfied with the existing state of art in any age is likely to produce anything very novel. Progress is usually the product of artistic discontent, though this does not infer that all progress is necessarily good—perhaps 'change' is a better word than 'progress.'

If people had for ever remained satisfied with the first 'organising,' what a curious world it would have been. But wonderful as these early efforts were, we owe a great deal to the thinkers who were not satisfied. Satisfaction is so dangerous in art. There ought to be no such thing, because a person who is satisfied with any result is incapable of seeing any further. So all honour to these thinkers.

From the knowledge we have of the attempts at elaborating 'organising,' we may gather that every system has had its adventurous experimenters.

Ex. 24 shows us Ex. 20 with another voice added by a comparatively modern writer, who was in close touch with the spirit of an earlier age. Though there is nothing particularly daring in this example, it is interesting to see what difference is brought about by the extra voice.

Soprano part added by BAINI (1775–1844).

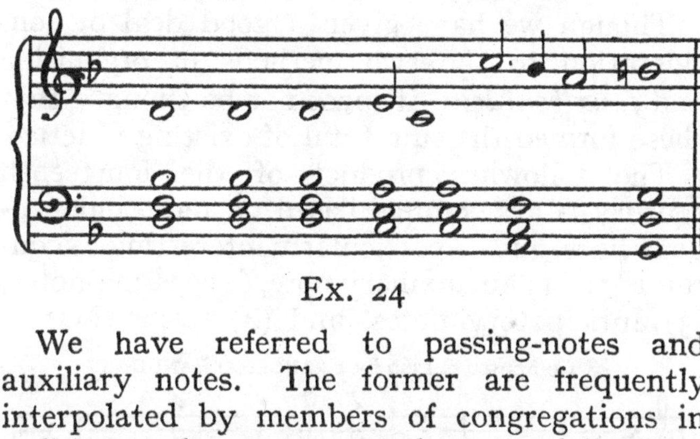

Ex. 24

We have referred to passing-notes and auxiliary notes. The former are frequently interpolated by members of congregations in well-known hymn-tunes such as the following:

Part of hymn, tune *Sun of my Soul.*

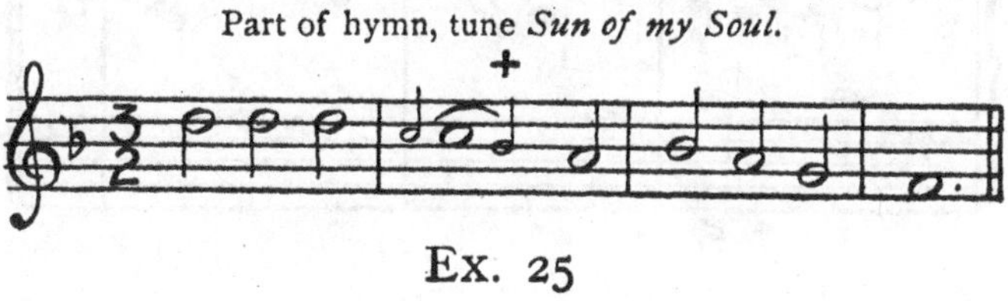

Ex. 25

an example sufficiently obvious to suggest how they were discovered.

Auxiliary notes, in the same way, owe their origin to the inherent human desire for ornamentation, and they play an important part in giving life to subjects which would otherwise be lacking in definition and crispness.

The *trio* of the *scherzo* in Beethoven's 7th Symphony is built almost entirely on the little figure where the auxiliary note C sharp adds the vivifying sparkle.

Though we have given a good deal of consideration to the two methods of organising and *faux-bourdons*, it must not be thought that these formed the sum-total of existing practice.

The following product of the fourteenth century is an example based on more independent lines, and is particularly interesting as containing: (1) an auxiliary note, (2) passing-notes, (3) anticipatory notes, and (4) suspensions:

Composed *c.* 1360 by FRANCESCO LANDINO.

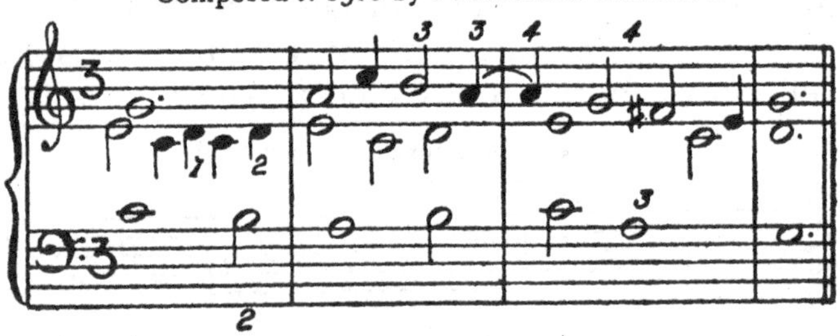

Ex. 26

Taking the following as the harmonic foundation :

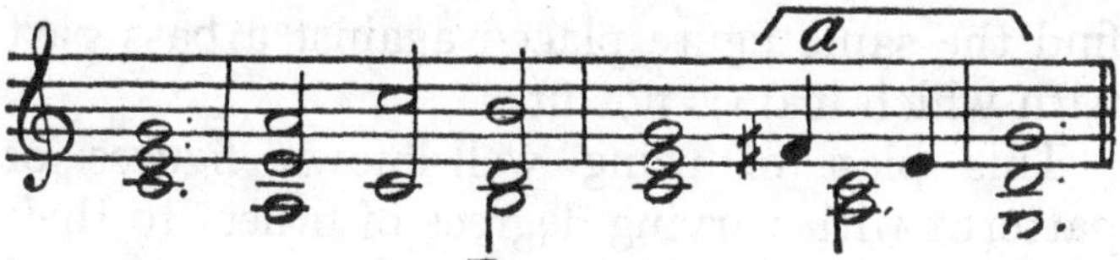

Ex. 27

it will be appreciated how the composer has elaborated it.

The last progression of this example marked *a*, was a very usual cadence, or close, during the period under notice. This is possibly due to the fact that it could be used successfully in most of the ancient modes, many of which had a tone, not a semitone as the seventh degree of the mode. So accustomed did people's easr become to this little melodic turn, that we find it cropping up in endless ways, even where it does not fit. The following extracts from Stainer's *Dufay and his Contemporaries* will serve as illustrations :

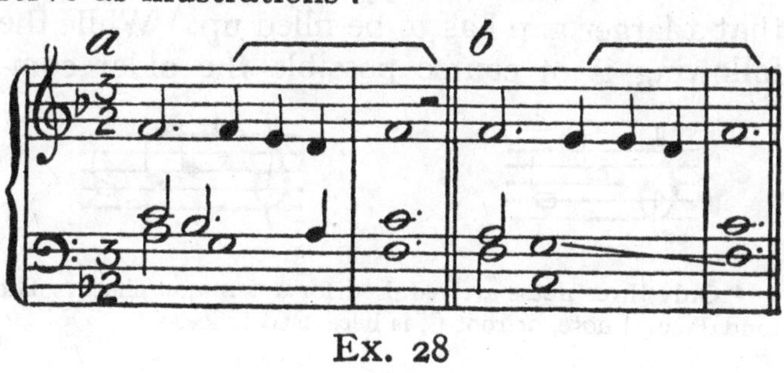

Ex. 28

In the extract *a* the tenor part reflects the treble with indifferent success, while in *b* we find the same figure placed against a bass part with which it does not fit.

This plan of using well-known figures or patterns with varying degrees of fitness to their surroundings is accountable for many novel progressions.

Another device known as *Nota Cambiata* was accorded similar treatment. If we examine this common chord[1] it will be seen that the lower three notes are each closer together than the upper two.

If we take these three notes as a descending passage we can fill in the 'gaps' with passing-notes thus :

but if we choose the upper two notes, we find that a larger gap has to be filled up. While the following is of course possible the older com-

[1] Only three notes are required for a common chord. The fundamental note, or root C, is here used twice.

posers, perhaps thinking this too skittish, preferred to use the following formula or *Nota Cambiata:*

Its peculiarity lies in the fact that the passing-note † is quitted, not as an ordinary passing-note which proceeds to its next-door neighbour, but by leap of a third in the same direction, eventually moving to the note above.

The classification of chords was unknown to the early contrapuntal writers. Long experience had taught them what were the best intervals to use above a bass note; but there was no system by which these resultant chords could be recognised as they are now by any student of harmony. Observance and perseverance eventually established a classification of intervals which, with one or two modifications, holds good at the present day. Above any bass note, the intervals of an octave, or a perfect fifth, were called *perfect concords;* thirds and sixths were *imperfect concords;* seconds, fourths, and sevenths, were counted as *discords.* The same classification held good in the compounds (p. 17) of all these intervals. Though the interval of a perfect fourth above a bass note is often met in harmony, the contrapuntal writers used it only if the note forming the interval had been ‘prepared’ or sounded in the previous chord. It was then treated as a suspension (p. 41) and required to be resolved on to the note below it.

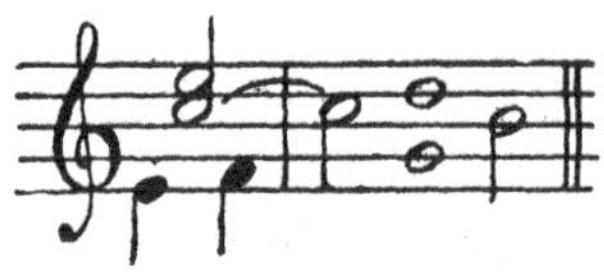

Taking a note C, and placing above it the concordant intervals, we obtain the following result :

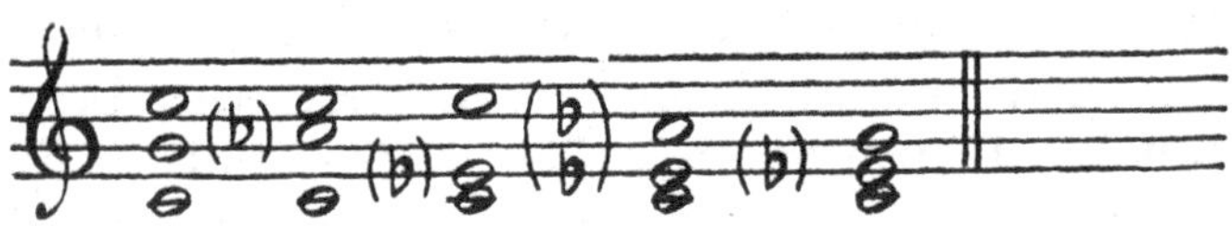

Ex. 29

The accidentals in brackets would be used in the minor mode. For the sake of saving space this example is written in three voice parts only, but it must be understood that more parts could be added to them by repeating, or doubling, one or more of the notes at the distance of an octave above.

Now, although each of these chords, according to its surroundings, has a distinguishing name in harmony, the old contrapuntal writers knowing nothing of ‘roots’ of chords (p. 70) used these vertical combinations of sound as the outcome of their classification of intervals above any given bass note.

It is interesting to observe that the chords resulting from contrapuntal practice agree with what may be termed 'common-chord' harmony excepting in one important instance, the explanation of which will require a short digression.

In terms of harmony  is called the common-chord[1] of C major in *root position,* because the note C, on which the chord is built, is in the bass or lowest part. When C is removed and placed above, thus:  the chord is in *first inversion.* If we cut away E and place it above, making G the bass-note, we produce the *second inversion* of the common-chord of C major.  This last chord, though freely used in harmony (and modern counterpoint), was counted a discord in the older counterpoint, because of the interval of a fourth between the bass note G, and the C. We have already shown how the early writers treated this interval.

A perusal of Ex. 29 shows that there is

[1] A common-chord consists of a note with a major or minor third, and perfect fifth, added above it.

therefore much truth in the statement, that the early writers used as a basis only chords which would now be called common-chords and their first inversions. On this simple foundation they built their compositions, elaborating them with the devices we have already explained. These were (1) suspensions, (2) anticipations, (3) passing-notes, and (4) auxiliary notes. The first of these ornaments occurred on the stronger accents; the three latter on the weaker portions.

From a Mass by JOSQUIN DE PRÉS (born *c.* 1450).

Ex. 30

The curious little figure on page 45, and *Nota Cambiata* have been mentioned.

This then was the technical outfit that sufficed to bring forth the writings of the great polyphonic masters of the period which culminated in Palestrina.

A comparison of the foregoing example with Ex. 26 will show the advance in freedom of writing wrought in a hundred years or so.

The smoothness and interesting movement of the voices are outstanding features. In passing it may be noticed that what in harmony would be called forms of the chord of the *dominant seventh* occur at the three marked points. These are all off the accent, and are merely the result of ornamentation.

The writers of the polyphonic school confined their efforts, speaking generally, to the notes of the scale or mode which they happened to employ; when what we should term 'modulation' took place, it was always the result of the movement of the parts. Tonality was not fully appreciated until the time when musicians adopted a chord with a major third built on the fifth degree of the scale or mode. This chord is now called the dominant chord. As many of the modes have a minor third above their fifth degree, it is clear that there could be no dominant chord, in a modern sense, without

PALESTRINA. *O Gloriosa Domina.*

EX. 31

Ex. 31 (*cont.*)

tampering with the modes by adding accidentals. This was not legal; moreover it took a long time for artistic requirements to prevail over theoretical enactments.

Chromatics, or notes not in the mode, were not employed; such a thing as:

was never used in serious works.

This kind of progression was not entirely unknown, however, for in the thirteenth century we find the following:

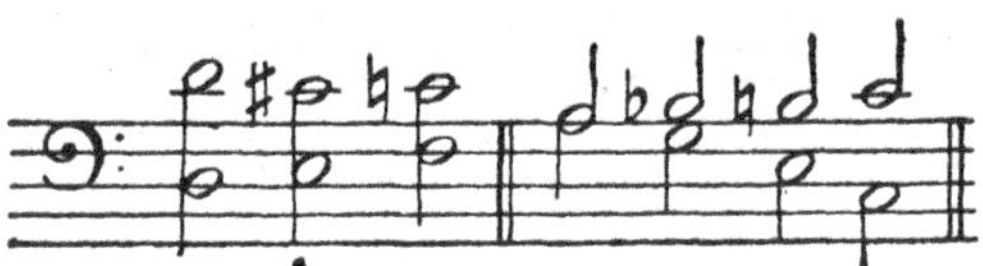

A

an example well outside the sphere of contemporary established practice.

This was too sensuous for the type of mind which was able to produce the example on pp. 52, 53—which is written for no less than twelve voices.

In this fine extract the harmonic basis is of the simplest description. The four bars represent glorified versions of four triads or common-chords, viz. C, G, D, G; but round these chords are woven most of the devices used by Palestrina. At A and B we meet with differing versions of the *Nota Cambiata* (p. 47); the version at B was possibly largely instrumental in preparing people for the sound of the chord of the dominant seventh as suggested by

PALESTRINA. *Se dai soavi accenti.*

Ex. 32

the note F. In the third bar there is a licence—which the composer has used in other works—for the rule is, that when the movement between parts stands out conspicuously, there must be harmonious agreement between these parts ; but here both kinds of fourths used (between the Alto of Chorus II and the Tenor of Chorus III) are discordant in strict counterpoint. When a composer sets himself the task of writing in twelve parts, these minor licences require small apology. In the third bar, the third chorus Soprano avoids the *Nota Cambiata* by filling in the gap with the note B. The manner in which the notes between a root and its fifth above are used is in evidence in this example, and is typical of Palestrina's style.

Though Palestrina placed the crown on this kind of contrapuntal writing, it is interesting to remember that long practice in that style of work had taught him to value upright combinations of sound for their own sake. He frequently wrote note-against-note as a contrast to his more elaborate work. The foregoing will serve as an example (Ex. 32).

CHAPTER V

THE DAWN OF MODERN HARMONY

WE have considered the technique which sufficed for the masterpieces of the polyphonic period. Though simple in foundation, from the harmonic point of view, many new chords[1] were foreshadowed by the use of passing-notes and other ornaments. Practically all of these chords, except those caused by suspensions, were on the weak portions of the music—not on the accents. As these unaccented combinations became familiar, they were transferred to the accented portions of music.

To Monteverde (b. Cremona, 1568) belongs the honour of the following, which must have been a veritable marvel when it appeared in 1599:

[1] The word ' chord ' is used to denote a discord as well as a concord—in fact any logical combination of notes. Any chord containing a note, or notes, outside a common-chord is a discord, because it requires to be followed by a chord of resolution.

MONTEVERDE. From Madrigal *Cruda Amarilli*, 1599.

Ex. 33

Here the composer boldly takes—in the treble voice—a ninth E and a seventh C above the bass, without any preparation. This was a great innovation, for, as we have already seen, these intervals had previously been used only as suspensions (p. 41). Whatever may be the view as to the chord, or vertical combination, on the second crotchet of the bar, there can be no doubt that the chord on the fourth crotchet is that of the *dominant seventh*, or dominant chord with a minor seventh added.

In due time the chord received its hall-mark of acceptance. When a chord has become thus established composers are not slow to exploit its possibilities. One favourite device is to transplant a chord to other degrees of the scale regardless of the alteration of the *quality* of the intervals forming the chord. The following will exemplify this :

CREYGHTON (b. about 1639). From anthem *I will Arise.*

Ex. 34

Here at *a* is an ordinary dominant seventh chord followed by a seventh built on the subdominant, or fourth degree of the scale. This particular progression became known as a ‘Creyghton seventh.’

In a lecture[1] the author has suggested three methods by which new chords have come into being : (*a*) *contraction*[2] — whereby a progression is brought about by omitting one or more steps ; (*b*) *expansion*[2]—where the result is obtained by adding steps which in themselves may have little to do with the first and last

[1] *Harmonic Thought : Past and Present* (delivered for the Royal College of Organists at Newcastle-on-Tyne, 1912), Messrs. Augener & Co.

[2] In Chapter VII these terms are also used, but with reference to the *size* of certain *chords*.

phases of the progression; (*c*) *chromatic distortion*—where the chords or units of a progression are chromatically altered, and sometimes so much so that they become diatonic chords of keys otherwise totally unrelated (*vide* Ex. 47).

In Ex. 34 the progression in question is probably the result of contraction, for in another work by the same composer we find the following:

CREYGHTON. From anthem *Praise the Lord.*

Ex. 35

the normal chord * being placed between the dominant and 'Creyghton' sevenths. The final cadence of this anthem is built on the same lines, but omits the Creyghton seventh, and another chord is placed above the bass note A flat (Ex. 36).

It is instructive to observe how with a general likeness of melodic contour in each voice in these three examples there are so many changes of harmony. The last five notes of the tenor voice are adjusted in three different

CREYGHTON. Final cadence of anthem *Praise the Lord.*

Ex. 36

ways. This practice of using some well-known melodic formula in connection with novel harmonic surroundings is productive of many new progressions in harmony.

Composers have long exhibited a tendency

KING. *Service in C.*

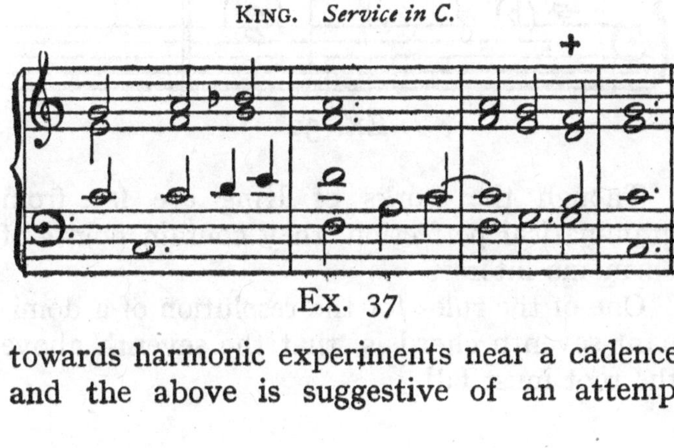

Ex. 37

towards harmonic experiments near a cadence, and the above is suggestive of an attempt to fuse the two chief cadences, (*a*) dominant to tonic, and (*b*) sub-dominant to tonic.

The curious result is a blend of some such formulæ as:

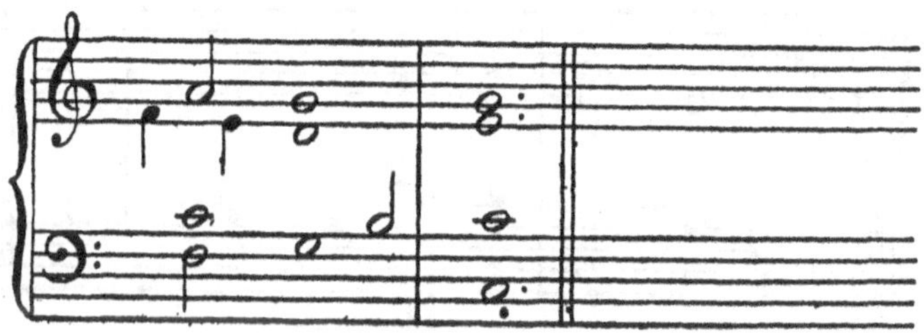

Ex. 38

and

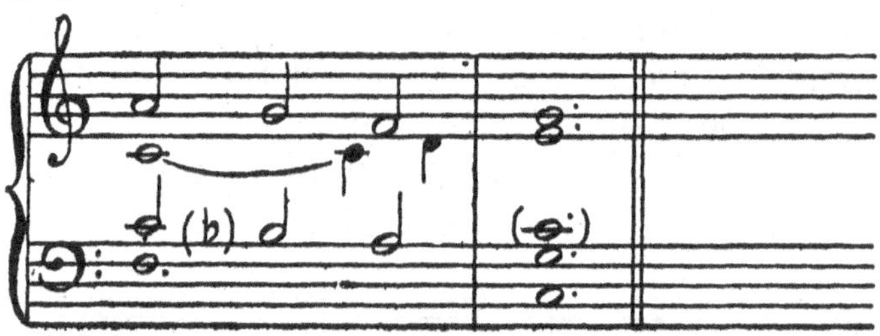

Ex. 39

Though the works of King are far from grammatical perfection, they contain points of harmonic interest.

One of the rules for the resolution of a dominant seventh chord is, that the seventh above the root must fall.

Among the barely acknowledged exceptions we find the following resolution :

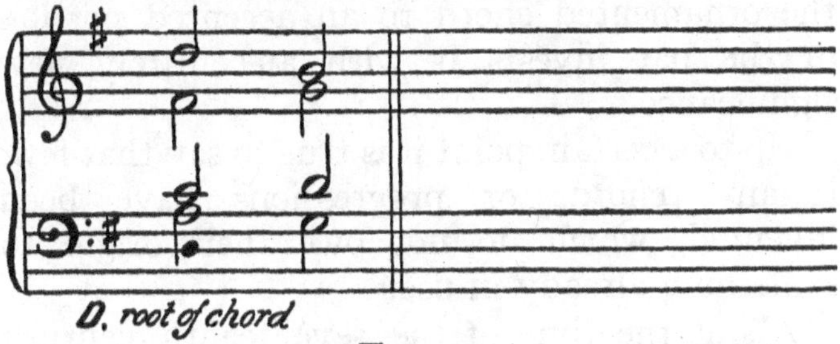

Ex. 40

C, the seventh above D (the root), being made to rise. In common with other contemporaries, King used the following :

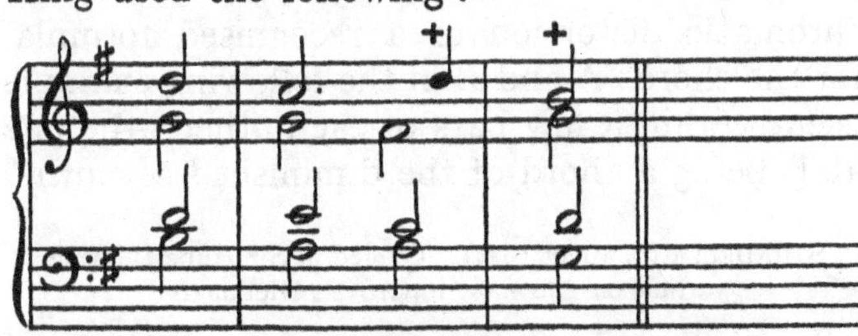

Ex. 41

At the chords marked + he thus produced, by means of an ornamental note the progression shown in Ex. 40, but with this difference—King's chord is not on the accent as is the case in Ex. 40. This small example is enough to furnish another instance of how new progressions are formed often by the ornamentation of a simple phrase at a weak portion of the accent. The subsequent transference of the ornamented chord to an accented portion of the bar invests it with an entirely new significance.

Up to a certain point it is true to say that few, if any, chords or progressions have been invented, which do not owe their origin to something already in use.

About the time of the seventeenth century composers were experimenting with, and continually altering, familiar chords or progressions. The introduction of the chord of the diminished seventh seems to have been the result of chromatic distortion of a recognised formula, for the chords A and B in the following example occur within a few bars of each other—the one at B being a chord of the diminished seventh.

STRADELLA (b. about 1645). Quoted in Sir Hubert Parry's article on *Harmony* in Grove's Dictionary.

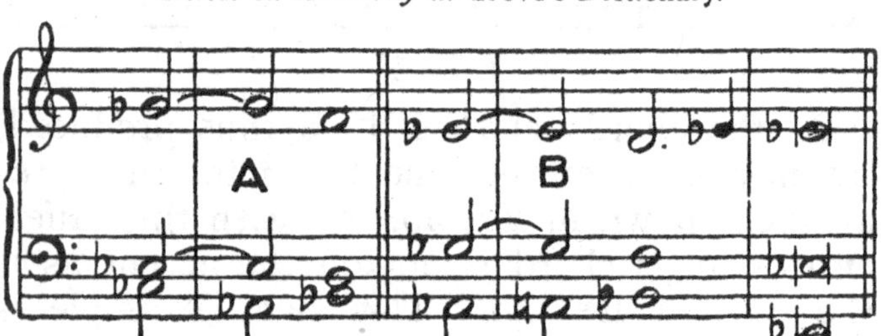

Ex. 42

This is perhaps the earliest case of its employment, though the skeleton chord marked A on page 54 has certain claims, for in actual composition the C sharp would probably be written as D flat, a diminished seventh above E.

The desire for dramatic expression has ever been a fruitful source of harmonic effects. In this respect, few have been prompted to a greater extent in the past than Henry Purcell (b. about 1658, d. 1695). His use of passing-notes was marvellous. It is the exception to find any passage of music written by him which does not exhibit harmony in its best contemporary guise, and in every way suited to the artistic requirements of the moment. When we remember that Bach and Handel were boys of about ten years of age when Purcell died, we begin to realise the prophetic genius of the great Englishman. Monteverde, by his use of unprepared discords, and such a chord as the diminished triad, i.e. a triad with a diminished fifth, had already broken new ground. To what extent Purcell was influenced by the daring Italian is uncertain. There is no doubt, however, that Purcell took full advantage of everything which tended to beautify and enrich his art, and the four following examples, all of them taken from the *Yorkshire Feast Song*, deserve careful notice.

Ex. 43

The chord at A is an augmented triad in its second inversion, and the striking passing-notes at B momentarily form a chord of the augmented sixth, if we imagine the F sharp to be changed to G flat. It is a remarkable effect for so early a date, and savours of Debussy in his whole-tone scale moments.

In the following twin extract we see further

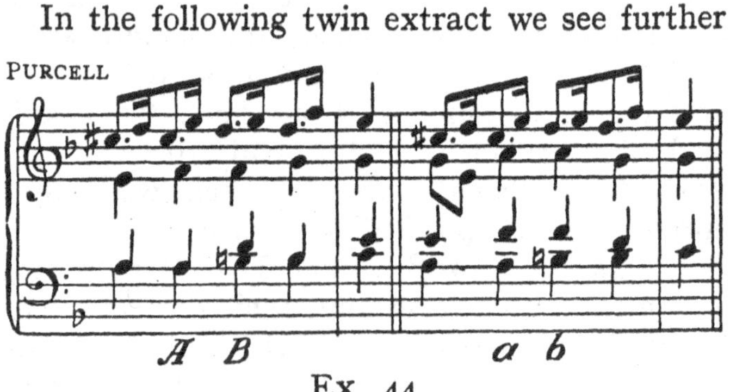

Ex. 44

use of the augmented triad at *A*, *a;* the diminished triad at *B* ; and what is known as a first inversion of a dominant ninth at *b*.

The freedom of Purcell's part-writing is further exhibited in Ex. 45, where at *a* the alto voice has a displaced note E, instead of F ; though it should be mentioned that the vocal

Ex. 45

bass part has E and D (quavers) on the first beat of the bar, against the orchestral crotchet D.

At *b* and *c* there is a persistent D in the tenor

voice. This device of sustaining a note against moving harmony is usually confined to the bass and is termed a *pedal*. For lack of a better definition, Purcell's example may be called an 'internal' pedal.

At *d* we meet with a good example of a somewhat unusual chord formed by passing-notes between two positions of the dominant seventh chord.

In the next example there is a chord at *a*, modern to a degree. When a note is sounded in close proximity to its own chromatic altera-

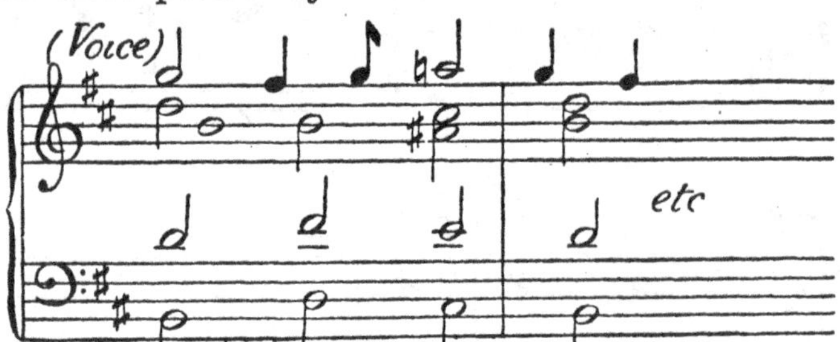

Ex. 46

tion, it is called a *false relation*. In the case under notice, two A's, one natural and the other sharpened, are actually sounded together, but the effect is beautiful. This is largely due to the fact that each part is moving on well-established melodic lines, and the ear is less shocked than if the chord were to be struck by itself. We shall refer to this chord later on.

With regard to the use of augmented and diminished triads there is a point in common which probably led to their first employment, namely, that of straining towards the next chord. We give two simple examples. Here are two common chords A, *a*, followed respectively by two others, B, *b*:

A B *a* *b*

Either, chromatic alteration, or the feeling after a certain scale, or dramatic instinct, or other stimulating cause, has in time produced the following obvious variations:

A B *a* *b* *

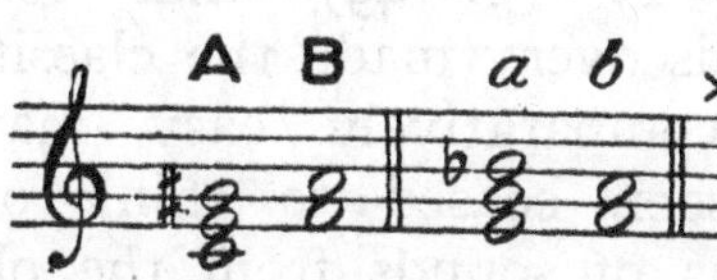

and the principle has been applied to other simple chords. For example, the following progression *A* has, by flattening the bass note, be-

* The combination at A is called an augmented triad; that at *a*, a diminished triad; the name in each case being derived from the quality of the fifth.

come the chord *B* at A, ultimately being enriched by the addition of a fourth note thus :—

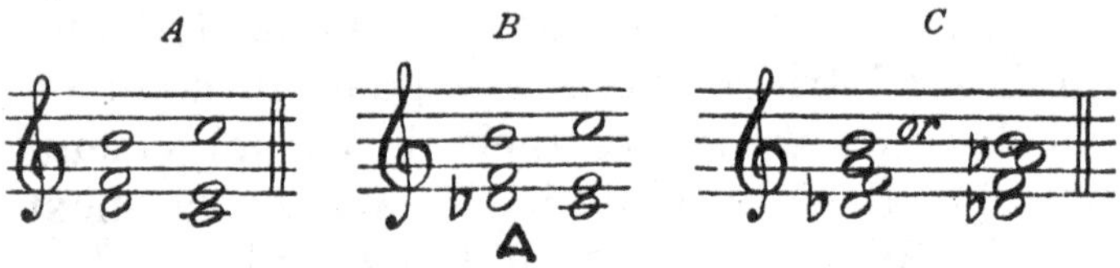

These combinations are known as the chord of the *augmented sixth* on account of that interval between the bass and the treble.

About the time of Purcell, when harmony was ever increasing in scope and variety, musicians began to take an added interest in its scientific bearing. Rameau (b. 1683) did great service by his discovery of the law of the inversion of chords ; i.e. the system under which certain combinations of notes are said to be referable to a certain root. We have seen in Chapter IV (p. 49) what this means. Rameau's discovery made the classification of chords a comparatively easy matter, and musicians soon ceased to think of vertical combinations of sounds from the old contrapuntal standpoint. It is possible, too, that the new outlook of harmony did much to discourage any lingering desire to write in the old Church modes.

At this time also Italy, as in the previous two or three centuries, produced many musicians who added their share to the sum-total of musical technique, all of which was fully welded together in the personality of J. S. Bach (1685–1750).

The outlook of Bach was a new one, and his practice constituted the real dawn of modern harmony; for though each of his immediate predecessors had helped in detail, it was left to Bach to incorporate the whole of their practice. This he did in such a manner as to foreshadow, either by suggestion or attainment, all the harmonic effects up to within the past few years, if indeed not up to the present day. For modern developments are, many of them, experimental sophistications of recognised harmonic idioms.

The older contrapuntal writers produced vertical correctness according to the laws of counterpoint and not from their knowledge of classified chords. On the other hand, Bach built his counterpoint on an underlying harmonic scheme. Thus it is that in Bach's music there are found numerous vertical combinations which never existed in earlier writings; firstly, because the earlier writers possessed a very limited harmonic vocabulary; and, secondly, because their harmony was the result of the simpler means we have already explained.

Bach, working on his presupposed framework of harmony, elaborated this with counterpoint, each thread of which seemed to pursue its own independent decorative scheme.

An examination of Ex. 17 will help us. If we pick out all the harmony notes of each hand in the first bar we have this result :

a dominant seventh chord built on D. A similar chord on G is in the second bar. Analysis shows that the composer has simultaneously elaborated the same chord in two different ways ; the right hand adopting a plan of filling in the gaps by means of passing-notes, while the left hand indulges in the broken harmony (Ex. 13) method of elaboration together with passing-notes. In the second bar the process is reversed in each hand.

Assuming the harmonic basis to be what we have mentioned, we find that notes belonging to the harmony are sounded together only on three beats of each bar, viz. at the first, second, and fourth quavers; and there is only one other place in each bar—the last semiquaver—where two harmony notes coincide.

This simple example is very instructive. It shows us that when composers had become accustomed to harmony, they were content to outline its characteristic features by means of counterpoint, though this elaboration did not necessarily fit in in strict detail, judged by the standard of the older writers.

It stands to reason too that many new vertical combinations resulted from this method of employing counterpoint. These would suggest fresh harmonic possibilities.

The device known as the *appoggiatura* was probably the result of a passing-note occurring on, not after, the beat. On referring to Ex. 17, it will be noticed that of the last four semiquavers in the first bar, three are harmony notes. Now, if we retain the right-hand part, and play the two left-hand notes together, adding the missing harmony-note F sharp, we arrive at the combination, which generally goes by the name of

a dominant thirteenth chord, as the note B is a thirteenth above D.

This *appoggiatura* device has produced endless harmonic varieties.

In the *Chromatic Fantasie* Bach uses the following, E flat being an appoggiatura. Wagner (1813–83) uses this appoggiatura chord as a recognised separate sound, and treats it thus in *Götter-Dämmerung*:

Many modern harmonic progressions are found foreshadowed in this and other ways in the works of Bach. In the 'Crucifixus' of the great Mass in B minor we find, as a result of the bass descending by semitones, the chord marked A:

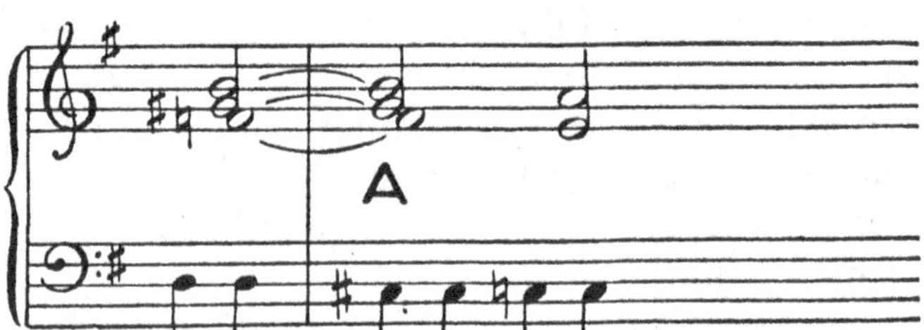

Ex. 47

This chord shows us how strongly both the contrapuntal and harmonic factors were welded in Bach's mind. From only the harmonic point of view perhaps Bach would never have thought of this astonishing chord; but coming as it does over a twelve-times repeated bass figure, he felt that the C sharp could be used contrapuntally as a chromatic passing-note, while at the same time his harmonic sense would appreciate the fact that the resultant chord was a well-known combination of sound, though with reference to another key-note. This exemplifies what was pointed out on page 8, viz. that many chords called new are only so in effect when used in connection with some new tonal centre.

If in this chord we substitute E sharp for F natural (a change of name without a change of note is called an *enharmonic* change), we have a chord of the dominant seventh in the key of F sharp. The temporary borrowing of chords from other keys, though in the first instance discovered fortuitously, is another fruitful source of modern harmonic effect. There are many instances, in more recent writers, of the use of this borrowed chord. S. S. Wesley (1810–76) in his *Te Deum* in E has the following version:

Ex. 47A

Though the contrapuntal elaboration of harmony brought about many novel passing effects in the works of Bach, it is true that he never exploited any of these discoveries, or ran them to death as so many composers are tempted to do. On the whole, he used a very simple basis, and it was to his mighty contrapuntal genius that his novel harmonic effects were mainly

attributable. To show how simple the basis was on which he worked let us take these two chords: few would see the 'angel in the marble' here. Yet from these little blocks of sound was formed, with the aid of passing-notes, the subject of the great organ *Fugue in G minor.*[1]

[1] The simple harmonic scheme of this subject does not exist in the theme of Reinken, which is stated to have been the influencing stimulus on Bach's imagination. Reinken's subject is comparatively loose, vague, and diffuse.

Ex. 48

It is the perfect mastery over both harmony and counterpoint that makes Bach so baffling. The simplicity of means to produce some of his richest harmonic effects is no less remarkable. It is doubtful whether any composer, even with all the accumulated practice of harmony at his disposal, would produce a finer harmonisation than the following extract from a chorale.

St. Matthew Passion. No. 31.

Ex. 49

It is now possible to see how large a debt harmony owes to counterpoint. We have shown how much of Bach's novel harmonic effect was the result of contrapuntal practice. As a sheer harmonic inventor Purcell was possibly superior to Bach, and it is a great pity that the works of the former did not have the good fortune to be edited, and the 'sketches' filled in, at a date when composers were still in touch with Purcell's distinctive idiom.

The step from the old contrapuntal school to that of the dawn of modern harmony was not so immeasurably great as some might imagine. The process was one dealing largely with the question of accent; for we have seen several cases where discords occur off the accent in the old writers. These have gradually been transferred to the accented portion of music, to be used in turn as starting-points for fresh contrapuntal elaboration. The process of development, then, lies in alternate layers of counterpoint and harmony.

The fresh chords introduced in the period under notice were the dissonant triads, and the chords of (*a*) all the sevenths, (*b*) the augmented sixth, (*c*) the dominant ninth and one or two other doubtful permanencies.

The desire for increased range of expression accounts for many chromatically altered forms of chords already familiar in diatonic and simple guise.

No survey of harmony would be complete without a brief reference to the methods employed in tuning a keyed instrument. There are two methods which concern European music. These are known as (1) *just intonation*, and (2) *equal temperament*.

Just intonation implies that the intervals are tuned in accordance with the natural scale. This method renders the remoter keys out of tune to an unpleasant degree. In fact, the more in tune the 'home' keys are, so much more out of tune are the distantly related ones. For this reason the system may be said to be dead so far as instruments with a keyboard are concerned.

On the other hand, equal temperament aims at obtaining a scale of twelve equal semitones, the actual attainment being largely dependent upon the skill of individual tuners. This system enables composers of 'keyboard' music to make excursions into remote keys, without any of the limitations imposed by the just intonation principle.

J. S. Bach is stated to have used equal temperament in tuning his own instruments, and it is probably known to most readers that his famous forty-eight preludes and fugues were designed for an instrument so tuned.

When equal temperament began to be generally used, it played a more important part in suggesting novel harmonic possibilities than is sometimes ascribed to it.

CHAPTER VI

MELODIC ORNAMENTATION—ITS INFLUENCE UPON HARMONY

THE reader will have gathered that ornamentation has played a most important part in the development of harmony. Passing-notes as used in the older contrapuntal writings produced novel vertical combinations on the weak accents. These combinations when 'passed by the censor' were duly transferred to the accented portions of music.

If we turn to Ex. 30, we find no less than three unaccented versions of the chord of the dominant seventh at the points marked +, viz.:

a and *c* represent the chord in root position, while *b* is a first inversion of the same chord; *c* is a complete four-note version, while *a* and *b* are incomplete, the notes B and D being absent respectively.

None of these combinations of sound were

used on an accent, or unprepared, until more than a century later. It is important to remember that the fructifying power of passing-notes is coincident with the whole history of harmony.

Again, suspensions were the means of extending the harmonic vocabulary; and though in the first instance the suspended note was heard in the previous chord, this formality was dispensed with in process of time, so that instead of writing

Ex. 50

a composer would feel justified in using the combination at A, without previously 'preparing' the discordant D in the same voice, with this result:

Ex. 51

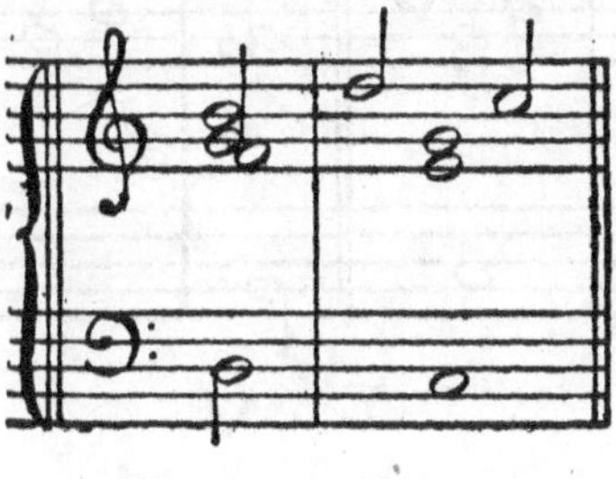

which was generally written

Ex. 52

This small note is called an *appoggiatura*, or 'leaning note,' and as we have already hinted, it has been highly productive of novel harmonic effects.

Before giving further examples of this ornament, we must refer to a twin companion, the 'retardation,' a term sometimes applied to a note which resolves upwards, as in the following two examples :

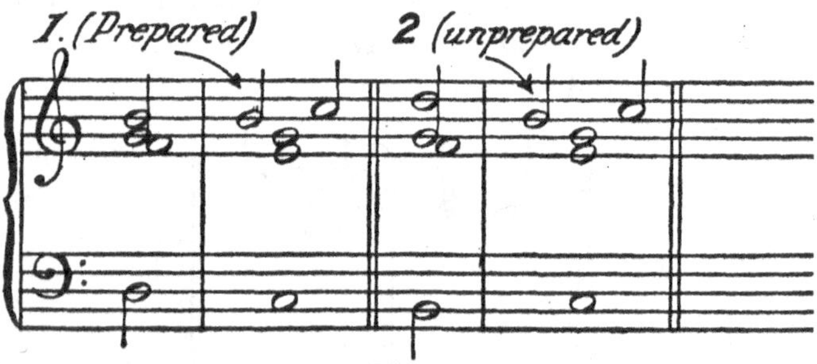

Ex. 53

It does not matter very much by what names these varieties of ornamental notes are known—appoggiatura, accented passing-note, auxiliary-note, or other designation—so long as the underlying principle is grasped, which is this : that a note may be temporally displaced by a note immediately above or below it. This displacement may take place *on* as well as *off* the beat. If the National Anthem were to be treated with these ornamental notes, we should have something like the following :

(The ornamental notes are marked +.)

Ex. 54

a treatment which of course robs the tune of

BEETHOVEN (Sonata No. 6).

Ex. 55

all its virility, though it serves to show how these notes can be used—or misused.

Ex. 55 furnishes us with instances of the ‘prepared’ kind.

The combinations at the points marked *a* are in the nature of suspensions, that at *b* is a retardation. Reduced to simple terms the right-hand part would read somewhat after this fashion :

Ex. 56

A further development of this practice of ornamentation is seen in the next extract :

BEETHOVEN (Sonata No. 5).

Ex. 57

which is a living piece of music founded on the dead model:

Ex. 58

By the insertion of the marked notes, Beethoven has transformed this, and the result is extremely instructive for our present purpose. The two notes marked + are, though struck again, in the same category as suspensions; those marked * are passing-notes; the other marked notes are displaced notes, or accented passing-notes. All of these marked notes are outside the harmony, and an important fact emerges, viz. that in bars 3 and 5 there is so much overlapping of the ornamentation, that very little of the real harmony remains at any one beat of the bar. Yet the framework of these bars is that shown in Ex. 58, and the ear accepts it as such in spite of the elaboration. It is now probably clear to the reader that every note has at least two 'satellites,' one above and one below. These satellites may temporally displace their parent note, and may be employed without previous preparation. Many well-known subjects derive their characteristics from the use of these satellites. The following is a case in point:

WEBER, *Rondo Brillante.*

Ex. 59

This is a mere ornamentation of

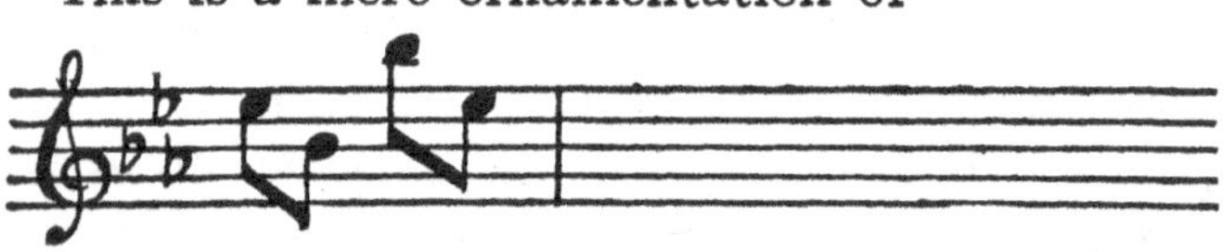

Ex. 60

and though the ornamentation in each case takes place before the accent, there would be theoretically nothing incorrect to write the subject as illustrated in Ex. 61, though of course this would no longer be what Weber wanted, as the theme thus loses its rhythmic snap and directness. This is caused by the harmony notes being transferred to the weak part of each beat.

Ex. 61

When these ornamental notes occur off the accent they do not attain to the same degree of expressiveness as when on the accent. Take the subject of the slow movement of Beethoven's first Sonata:

Ex. 62

and alter it thus by displacing the ornamental portions:

Ex. 63

the whole character is changed—much for the worse so far as expression is concerned.

The desire for the harmonic expression of dramatic instinct has led to the extensive use of these ornamental notes, and there are few better-known instances of their successful employment than in the following extract :

WAGNER (*Tristan and Isolde*).

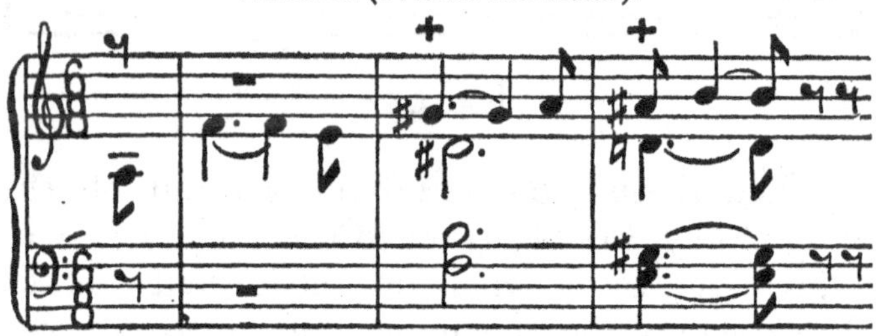

A.

Ex. 64

Here again, if we remove the marked notes from the accents we obtain this washy result :

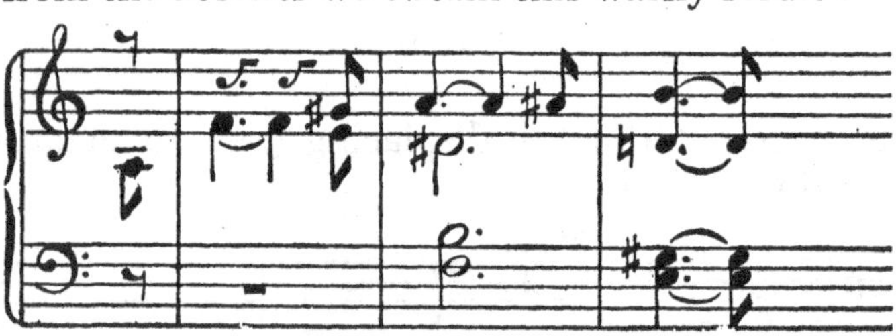

Ex. 65

and if we omit them we arrive at something approaching sheer nonsense.

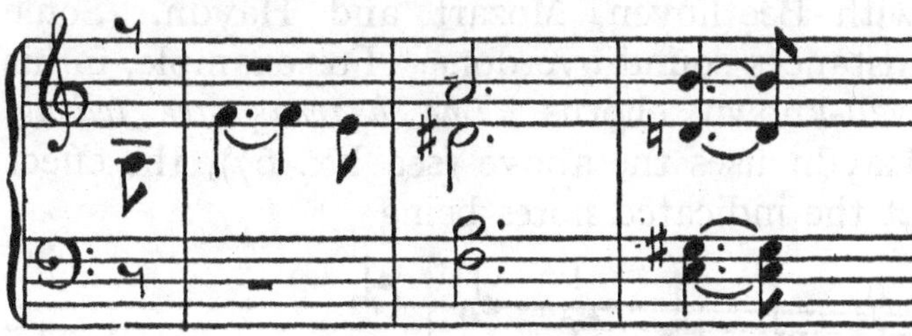

Ex. 66

Now, it is by the use of these ornamental notes in melody, in the first instance, that so many new effects have been obtained.

The chord marked A in Ex. 64 is doubly interesting, for it is a chromatic distortion of a chord (the augmented sixth) which is itself a distortion of a simpler chord (p. 70).

The plan of employing a simple melody in one voice, and a simultaneous elaboration of it in

Ex. 67

another voice or part (e.g. Ex. 55) was at one time fairly common, being a favourite device with Beethoven, Mozart and Haydn. Some instances sound overdone. For example, in his well-known chorus, *The heavens are telling*, Haydn uses the above (see Ex. 67), the effect at the indicated notes being

Ex. 68

which is distinctly on the harsh side. This is, however, an extreme instance. The practice of sounding a note together with one of its satellites at such close quarters is not now usually followed.

We will give one other example of the use of

SCHUMANN (*Op.* 12).

Ex. 69

ornamental notes, and show how the entire character of the subject would be altered were these omitted.

The elimination of the ornamental notes would leave us with nothing but the common chord of D flat, thus :

Ex. 70

In Ex. 69 there is enough going on in the left-hand part to guide the ear as to what chord is intended, and the unessential notes stand out distinctly as such. This is not always the case, particularly when a chromatic chord is concerned ; for it often happens that the distortion of such a chord throws the mind off the central note for the time being (a favourite modern device) by producing combinations of sound which refer to another key centre.

We have seen in the Bach extract (Ex. 47) an enharmonic form of a dominant-seventh chord in F sharp, due to the fact that the composer was working on a fixed bass part. Had this not been so, he would probably have written the following comparatively ordinary progression :

Ex. 71

and we should have lost one of the most beautiful chords in the movement.

In Ex. 64, too, Wagner produces a well-known combination of sound at A, but with reference to a key very remotely connected, viz. E flat.[1]

Ex. 72

Of course these are not the only possible ways of judging the mental effect of these

[1] This by enharmonic change, i.e. G sharp = A flat, D sharp = E flat, B = C flat.

chords, but the chords in Exs. 47 and 64 are sufficient to show how far the ear may be upset by the alteration of one note in a chord. The practice of altering notes seems to have first appeared in the melody. In turn it spread to other parts, and in process of time sometimes a whole chord would be altered. This we will consider in the next chapter. Meanwhile we may recall the fact that numberless novel harmonic efforts have been gained by the use of ornamental notes applied to separate voice-parts. It is important to remember, too, that these ornamentations have in the first instance usually occurred round some well-known chord. In many cases, these ornamented chords have already become absorbed by established practice. The ornaments of one generation become the essentials of the succeeding era.

CHAPTER VII

CHORD ORNAMENTATION

In the previous chapter we saw how the alteration of one note of a chord can impart an entirely different atmosphere. The practice which began with such simple melodic ornaments as the appoggiatura, for instance, did not long lack development. The principle soon

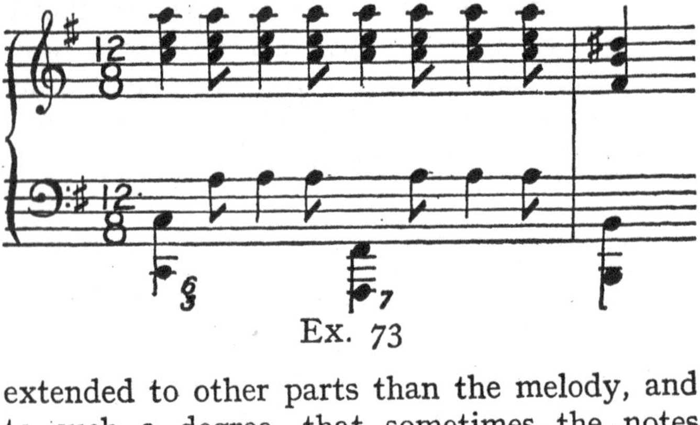

Ex. 73

extended to other parts than the melody, and to such a degree, that sometimes the notes forming a whole chord would be temporally displaced.

We can go back to early days for a very good

example ; for the contrapuntal mind of Bach was ever making use of unessential notes—practically whole chords of them.

An ordinary-minded person might have written such a piece of music as the foregoing, which in terms of harmony would be described as a six-three chord on C, followed by a chord of the seventh on F sharp, the latter chord resolving on a chord of B major.[1]

By the use of unessential notes—satellites—Bach, towards the end of the great first chorus in his *St. Matthew Passion Music*, has transformed this simple passage into one charged with the deepest expression.

Technically speaking, all the marked chords

Ex. 74

[1] It should be mentioned that C remains mentally the bass until F sharp is struck. Similarly F sharp is the true bass for the rest of the bar.

are formed from notes lying immediately above or below the notes of the principal chords ; and that Bach used the chords shown in Ex. 73 as his basis is sufficiently proved by the fact that he supplied figures in the full-score denoting such an intention.

The system of describing chords by placing figures below the bass, was known, though not generally adopted, nearly a century before Bach's time : and though the practice is now confined to useful purposes in teaching harmony, it has played an important, artistic rôle in the past. Composers took advantage of the system, and often wrote nothing but the bass, duly figured. This was done in contrapuntal music as well ; so that now we have no means of knowing how the composer wished to 'fill in' the parts, for idioms change. From the consequences of this convenient system of figures we still suffer, in not being able to reproduce many standard works exactly as the composers intended. A great point in favour of the system was that it incited imaginative skill on the part of performers.

The figuring used by Bach nearly always denotes a simple harmonic basis, and it is most instructive to see how he elaborates almost the same underlying harmony with contrapuntal effects of the most varied order. We thus deduce the fact that composers do not as a rule invent their new effects straight off, but usually have in their mind some simple formula which they deliberately deck with ornament. In Benjamin Dale's fine piano *Sonata in D minor* there are many examples of chord ornamentation, of which the following is a case in point:

B. J. DALE (*Sonata in D minor*).

Ex. 75

The parent chords of this example are roughly set forth in Ex. 76, and from them the reader can see what are the ornamental, i.e. unessential, notes, or notes outside the harmony, in Ex. 75.

Ex. 76

The chord which we saw in Ex. 47 has been added to by Strauss in his *Symphonia Domestica;* the following reduced extract shows this addition to the chord in the form of a minor ninth. For convenience of comparison the example is transposed.

Ex. 77

We have suggested more than once, that chords which are at first sight difficult to explain, are generally developments of a simpler idiom.

We will give an illustration showing some sophistications of the well-worn cadence sub-dominant to tonic. This, by the way, is known as the *plagal* cadence (*a*) of the following example):

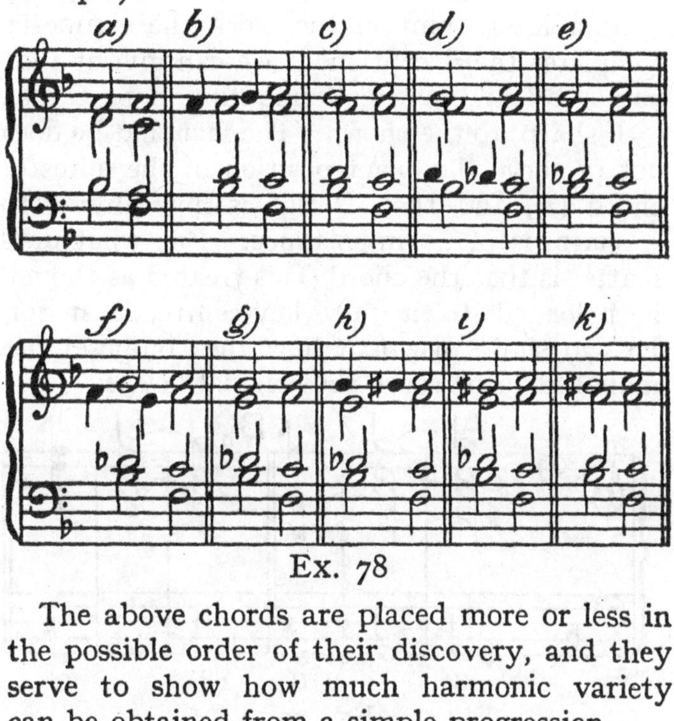

Ex. 78

The above chords are placed more or less in the possible order of their discovery, and they serve to show how much harmonic variety can be obtained from a simple progression.

The variety marked (*i*) has been much used by Strauss in a well-known orchestral work, and affords another instance of a chord becoming, by chromatic distortion, referable to

another key-centre. By substituting C sharp for D flat, and A sharp for B flat, we have this chord, generally known as a first inversion of the dominant-ninth chord in B major.

At a later point in the work the composer completes the deception, if we can give it that name, by adding the foundation note G flat (=F sharp) to the chord. The fact that he does not preserve the exact position of the notes of chord (*i*), and that D flat is now altered to C sharp, is of no importance. But what does matter is that the chord (*i*) is treated as though it belonged to a new key-centre, B major. Ex. 79 shows us at A how the composer has managed to preserve the original key, F.

Ex. 79

Shorn of its chromatic adornment the progression is nothing more than that shown in Ex. 79 at B. But we must take into consideration the fact that the composer had already used, many times, the right-hand chord notes of Ex. 79 A in the form of chord (*i*) in Ex. 78; and though the two portions of Ex. 79 possess similar points, the portion A did not start out in life with the intention of bearing any relationship to its prototype in the B portion.

This borrowing of chords from distantly related keys—looking round the corner—is, as we have hinted, a common modern device. The keyboard of a piano is without doubt a source of inspiration to composers. The 'feel' of a chord on any keyed instrument imprints itself on the mind; and as so many chords are almost the same in shape or feel, yet not in every detail, it often happens that a composer-pianist hits upon some subtle analogy between chords belonging to widely separated tonalities. Sometimes it is one note which makes all the difference; and sometimes an almost complete distortion of the chord by means of satellites, i.e. ornamental notes. Occasionally the strange effect is brought about by means of some foreign chord, whose notes lie within vocal or instrumental hail of a very ordinary progression or chord.

The sheer force of progress and the desire for increased power of human expression lead to new discoveries. There is a tendency, when some new chromatic combination is discovered

DALE (*Sonata in D minor*).

Ex. 80

which takes on the shape of a chord in another key, to treat this combination with all the ornaments of the foreign tonality. In other words, chords which are chromatic or foreign to the key, are often embellished according to the key which they temporally ape.

A reference to Exs. 47, 47 *a*, and 77, will make this clearer. We suggested the possible origin of Bach's chord in Ex. 47. Wesley in Ex. 47 *a* makes a slightly different resolution of the chord. Strauss in Ex. 77 uses the chord with the addition of a minor ninth, and makes an ornamental resolution.

As we are dealing with these kindred progressions for our immediate examples, we will give as the last of the series a still further ornamental chord built on the major third of a minor key (Ex. 80).

A great deal might be said about this chord, for it is full of instruction. In the first place it may be taken as a highly-organised distortion of the more ordinary progression in Ex. 81.

Ex. 81

This is in turn evolved from (*a*) in Ex. 82, or its more 'mody' relative (*b*), which is an accented version of (*c*) at the marked chord.

Ex. 82

Though this is a conveniently simple explana tion it is neither a sufficient nor a complete one. Another and probably a more satisfactory explanation is this: the C natural in the second bar of Ex. 80 is merely a satellite of B flat (=A sharp) on to which it resolves. That being granted, the note C need not be counted as essential to the chord, which now becomes the same that Strauss uses in Ex. 77 with a minor ninth in place of the major ninth of the Dale extract.

Thus we are able to trace the prototype of this complicated sound back to the days of Bach; at the same time we may make the chord serve as an apology for some remarks, partly of a scientific, and partly of an æsthetic, nature.

It is as well to mention that these two aspects have more in common than is usually supposed ; there is nearly always some scientific reason for the acceptance or rejection of an æsthetic principle.

When the old writers refused to finish a composition with a common-chord containing a minor third, they were perhaps unknowingly paying tribute to science, or, rather, the laws of nature. By referring to page 107 it will be seen that a major third is one of the early harmonics of a note. In certain dispositions of voices, a chord containing no third would supply a feeble major third of its own ; and it is this weak artificial major third that prevented early composers from using a minor third in the final chord. If we play the minims of the following example, we are able, when the sound settles down, to hear the note A shown as a crotchet:

Ex. 83

On some instruments we can still hear the ghostly A natural, or a jarring sound, round A flat of the chord in Ex. 84.

Not only notes throw off harmonics, but

harmonics themselves in a less degree throw off their own series of harmonics; all the aliquot parts of a vibrating medium add their quota to the general effect. In proportion as the distance upwards from a note increases, so the number of harmonics becomes greater.

Ex. 84 

From this fact it may be judged what a very complicated sound even a single note is. When more than one note is sounded the complication increases, as we shall see presently.

Some of the harmonics at the high end of the series seem to have little connection with those at the low end; they are quite outside the common-chord given us by the first four harmonics. Readers who wish to pursue this matter further should study Ex. 85 carefully; the example shows the first nineteen harmonics of the foundation note C.

Though the numbering of this example reaches twenty, only the nineteen black notes are harmonics. The note marked I is the foundation note which when sounded throws off the black notes as harmonics. The black notes with stems are more or less out of tune.

The figures under the notes show the ratio of vibrations; e.g. for every vibration of the foundation note 1, the note marked 2 will have two vibrations; and, to give another example, the note 12 will have twelve vibrations for every eight of number 8 note. These figures tell us that the vibration ratio of an octave is 1 to 2, and the ratio of a perfect fifth 8 to 12,

Ex. 85

or in this latter—reducing the figures to their lowest terms—2 to 3. In the same manner the ratios of other intervals may be discovered.

In addition to harmonics being thrown off by single notes, there are other sounds produced when two notes are struck simultaneously; the combined vibrations produce what is termed a *summational* tone, and the difference of their vibrations produces a *differential* tone. For example, if notes 2 and 3 in Ex. 85 are sounded together, we should hear note 5 as a summational tone; and the difference between the vibrations of notes 2 and 3 should give us a suggestion of note 1 as a differential tone.[1]

In passing it may be mentioned that these differential tones have been turned to useful account by organ-builders, for by means of two comparatively small pipes it is possible to obtain the effect of a note produced by a large pipe. As the large pipes are expensive a great saving is effected by using two small pipes as substitutes, but the note thus artificially produced by the two pipes is certainly inferior in resonance to one produced by a single pipe made for the same note.

Before going further we will make a little list of the three matters we have just discussed:

1. Harmonics,
2. Summational tones,
3. Differential tones.

We have considered it advisable to give a short description of these, for they often suggest scientific reasons for harmony which is apparently based on æsthetic principles only. Modern French and other writers have experimented largely with the scientific possibilities of harmony. Many readers will remember the later pieces by Debussy. That very original

[1] In trying this on a piano it will be found more convincing if the notes are played an octave lower.

composer is said to have taken observations from the overtones, or harmonics, of bells and bugles.

Though the artistic employment of these harmonics in actual composition is not yet fully developed, it would be unwise to ignore, and ungracious to belittle the honest efforts which have been made to enlarge the sphere of legitimate harmony.

Whether some of the strange notes, foreign to the harmony, are regarded as harmonics or as summational tones does not matter very much; but all those who play music of the modern French school, for example, will agree that almost the entire effect of these extraneous notes depends upon their being sounded with just the right amount of strength. They are felt by the composer (who usually marks them *pppp*) to be 'spicy'—a very good term, for spice, though not one of life's necessities, may enliven a dull dish.

Endless experiments can be made by playing Ex. 85 first as it stands, starting *ff* and ending *pp*, keeping down the sustaining pedal throughout. It will prove interesting if an attempt is made to give just the right amount of emphasis to those notes which are outside the common-chord of C major. Three players can play all the notes at once, without the aid of the sustaining pedal, but it will be difficult to give the proper degree of loudness to each note, some of which notes, it must be remembered, are not strictly in tune.

While on the subject of experiments we may point out that it is possible to play tricks upon the ear. For instance, we have seen how the harmonics of a note gather in number at the upper end of the series; in fact it seems as though almost any notes could be played high

Ex. 86

up on the piano, if there were sufficient harmonically logical support below them. This may not read like a very artistic statement; but there is little doubt that when the extreme limits of hearing are put to the test simultaneously, the ear can be deceived. If the reader will play the above (Ex. 86) he will find it sounds perhaps not as bad as it looks.

After playing the first two bars two or three times, play the chords following ; the trick is at once apparent when the sounds pass into normal regions. Bossi has worked out this idea in his *Satire Musicale*.

It is worth mentioning that if the right-hand part is played a semitone below instead of above the proper key (A) the trick no longer succeeds. The fact is interesting and may bear some analogy to the development of certain chords in harmony, such, for example, as the chord of the augmented sixth, which is felt to be a strained version of an ordinary chord of the sixth. For the Dale example (80) we have suggested an 'unstrained' version in Ex. 81, where the harmonies are contained in a space one semitone less than in Ex. 80.[1] Many more cases might be cited where chords, apparently expanded or strained, could be reduced to normal terms by eliminating certain accidentals.

The same might be said of those chords which are contracted by accidentals.

Though the author has not arrived at any very convincing conclusion, he is inclined to think that more new chords have been discovered by expansion than by contraction.

[1] *Vide*, p. 104, however, for what we consider a better explanation of the chord.

We have shown that harmonics, and perhaps summational tones, have been used by composers; we will now give two curious examples of cadences in which these are employed. The first is from Ravel's *Sonatine*, the second from the same composer's *Jeux d'Eau*, both written for the piano (Ex. 87).

Here the G sharp in the chords marked 1 is the extraneous note; it is scientifically explained by its being a harmonic of C sharp, and æsthetically justified in proportion as it is appreciated by the hearer, or presented by the player, as a balanced artistic effect. The chord marked 2 is made up of notes, or satellites, lying round the notes of the common-chord of the key, F sharp.

The series of consecutive fifths in the left-hand bears analogy to the artificial low notes produced on organs (*vide* p. 108) and serves as an instance of the use of implied differential notes, though naturally there is a great dissimilarity between implying and actually sounding a note. It must also be said that the composer has taken risks at the beginning of the passage, as the music lies in range of the most easily distinguishable part of the piano; also, the chords are 'spaced' normally. We shall refer to the subject of spacing later on.

Ex. 87

As to Ex. 88 we will content ourselves with the statement that D sharp (in place of E) is a strong harmonic of G sharp, which is the third of the chord, and the experiment is carried more into the range of hearing where tricks succeed.

Ex. 88

In Chapter I we said that some composers had founded systems on which they built their harmony. The scope of the present work does not allow more than a passing mention of these methods to be made, and in choosing perhaps the best-known and most easily grasped of them we pass over the methods of Schönberg and Scriabin in favour of the so-called whole-tone scale which has been much used by Debussy[1] and other writers.

The reader is already aware of the fact that

[1] Though the whole-tone scale is usually associated with the name of Debussy, its effect was known and used before his time.

passing-notes have added many new chords to music. When a new chord is discovered, it is soon treated with the embroideries given to older-established combinations of sound. The ordinary augmented triad has been ornamented in this manner. Already we have seen how Purcell in Ex. 43 has fitted out an augmented triad with passing-notes. If he had used an A flat he would have completed the whole-tone scale.

A little explanation of this scale is necessary. It is a scale which is built on the supposition that all the notes of a piano are equidistantly separated from their neighbours ; this implies that the alternate notes are also equidistant. The whole-tone scale then is one which proceeds regularly by each alternate note on the piano. The principle sounds easy in theory, but as a matter of practice a scale consisting entirely of tones cannot be written without introducing intervals which are quite beyond the pale of practical harmonic effect. Let us, for example, write a scale of tones from C and we have the following result :

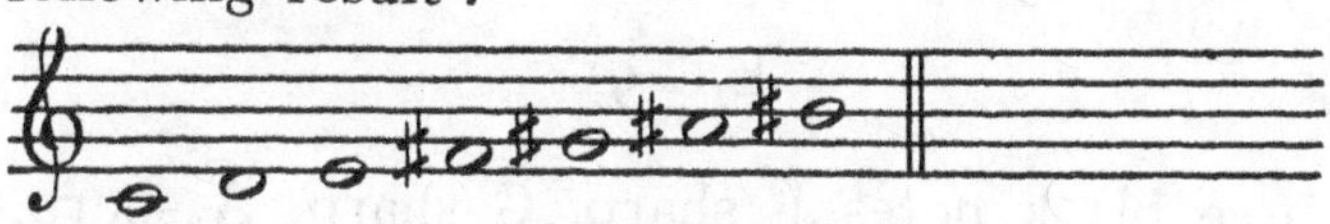

Ex. 89

giving us an augmented seventh from C to B sharp—an unheard-of interval in music. In actual practice, the necessity of reaching the octave in six moves (due to the omission of the semitones between the third and fourth, and seventh and eighth degrees of a normal major scale) is met by the makeshift of writing a diminished third at one point of the so-called whole-tone scale. Ex. 90 shows this.

Ex. 90

Perhaps in years to come, in using this scale, composers will adopt some simpler method of writing down their works.

A little thought shows us that there are only two possible sets of tones on the piano keyboard, namely: (1) scales formed from the

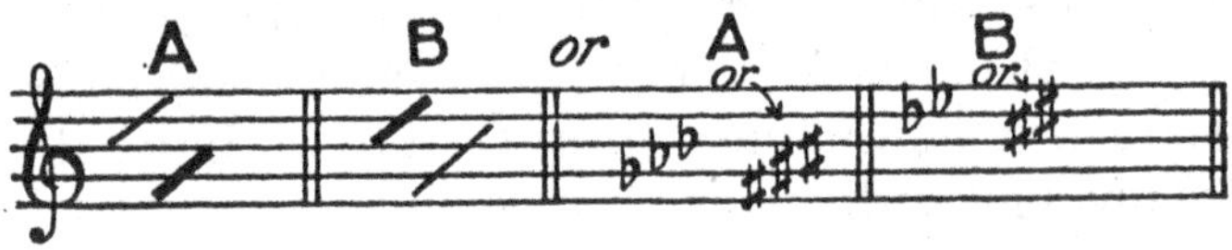

Ex. 91

three black notes F sharp, G sharp, A sharp, and three white notes C, D, and E; or (2) scales formed from the two black notes C sharp and D sharp, and the four white notes F, G, A, and

B. For the former series we would suggest some such key-signature as is shown in Ex. 91 at A; and for the second series, the signature in the same example at B.

The whole-tone scale is an instance of the varied experiments made in dividing the octave into equal intervals. The division into semitones is perhaps the one now most exclusively used, and composers have come to regard all the notes of a chromatic scale as of equal availability for harmonic purposes. The division into alleged tones gives us a scale of six notes; the division into minor thirds gives us four notes, forming the diminished-seventh chord; the division into major thirds gives us an augmented triad, from which it is easy to trace the whole-tone scale.

To make this clearer we give in Ex. 92 an augmented triad on C.

Ex. 92

The embellishment of the chord would suggest itself in the use of the passing-notes D and F sharp; and the difficult gap between G sharp and the upper C would be filled in by the note lying two semitones above G sharp on the piano, or two semitones below C. We cannot write this note without producing a diminished third between it and G sharp or C, for if we use B flat there is a diminished third above G sharp, and if we use A sharp instead, we have a diminished third below C. It is of course absurd to use B sharp instead of this C, for we should have to start from there with a fresh set of complicated notes such as is shown in Ex. 93.

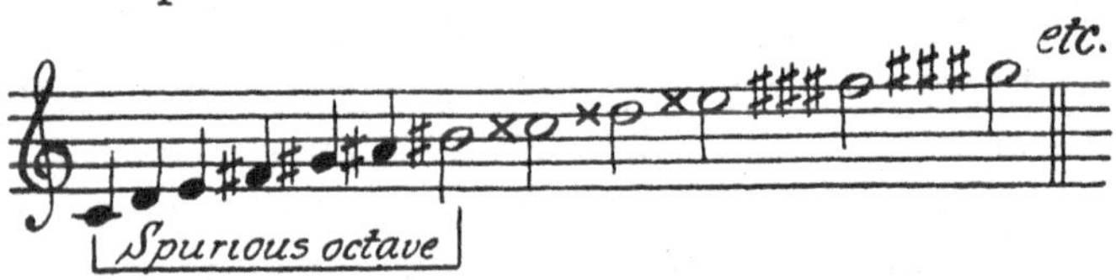

Ex. 93

As there are seven letters used in music, and there are only six notes in the whole-tone scale, those who have made use of this scale have settled the matter by the compromise of a diminished third, shown in Ex. 90. We will now give a little attention to the employment of this scale, which in some respects is like an *arpeggio*, for all the notes of the scale can be sounded simultaneously provided they are 'spaced' properly. Spacing is the art of presenting a chord in its most intelligible form, and in general terms it implies that notes which are discordant with each other should not be crowded together but should be allowed space or 'elbow-room,' so that their individual value in the general effect may be properly assessed.

A familiar example will make this clearer. The following is an ordinary diatonic chord (Ex. 94 at *a*), made up of no less than five consecutive notes of the major scale of C, a combination which would sound both hideous and meaningless were it not spaced properly. (Ex. 94 at *b*.)

Ex. 94

A chord with every note of the diatonic scale is shown in Ex. 94½.

The important part which the system of spacing plays in modern harmony cannot be overestimated; perhaps between that system and the absurd little trick shown in Ex. 86 there may be something in common which makes it possible for the ear to tolerate chords or combinations which would otherwise be incomprehensible.

Ex. 94½

We will now give an example in the whole-tone scale. The chord in Ex. 95 at (*a*) would be quite ordinary among consistent surroundings, while at the same time it would be nonsense were all the notes played bunched together as at (*b*) of the same example.

Ex. 95

Such a scale as this, of course, upsets all ideas of tonality or key-centre; consequently its use will always be restricted to the portrayal of subjects which are not intended to be thrust at the listener. The harmonies derived from the scale are intangible and picturesque rather than weighty or impelling.

It may be mentioned in connection with scales that the Indians possess no fewer than seventy-two differently constructed scales. Our major scale is the fifty-fourth of their series. The employment of this vast array of scales, however, is confined to the varying of melodic, not harmonic, resource. Sir Alexander Mackenzie makes use of some of these Indian scales in his oratorio *Bethlehem*, a work in which of course there is the enrichment of harmony.

Returning to the chord in Ex. 80 let us see whether we can understand it from other points of view now that we have examined a few of the developments of modern harmony. It we dispose of the C sharp in the left-hand part, for instance, we have remaining a five-note chord of a whole-tone scale on F sharp. If we look upon the first triplet in the left hand as two fifths on two F's sharp, we may with a grain of faith regard it as representing a sound equal to a plain F sharp, thus eliminating the C's sharp, for the 'differential' of each fifth is a sound an octave lower than the lower note of each fifth This may be a far-fetched explanation, but it is one entitled to consideration in view of what has been said in this chapter.

After one more explanation we will 'worry'

this chord no more. We have purposely analysed the chord from more than a single standpoint, as it appears to be a kind of connecting link between several of the subjects we have discussed.

We have mentioned the *contraction* of chords. If we regard the C natural as C sharp displaced a semitone the chord is at once transformed, with a C sharp, into an ordinary major ninth on F sharp. This progression has already been noticed. The substitution of C natural instead of C sharp, under the head of the present explanation, can only be partly excused by 'ear-tricks' and effective 'spacing.'

If we admit the possibility of C natural as a substitute for C sharp we should have an instance of a *contracted* chord, i.e. a chord filling a smaller space than it would fill in normal guise. We still, however, adhere to the more likely explanation on page 104.

In concluding the present chapter we wish to refer the reader to the Purcell extract in Ex. 46.

It should be mentioned that the top part is written for a tenor voice, which of course sounds an octave lower than the written notes. This causes the A sharp and A natural to be sounded in the same octave; but as the accompaniment is for strings—a different quality of tone—that fact need not disturb us so very much. As it stands, with the A natural at the top, the chord is quite a well-known modern combination, and serves to show how ornaments become essentials in process of time.

The principle adopted by Purcell may be described as one of delayed resolution, though this is only one of many possible explanations. The A natural is a displaced note, G, attained by melodic impetus. Instead of falling to G the real note of the chord, for the second half of the minim thus,

Purcell delays the operation till the following bar. He is thus perhaps the first user, and a very bold one at that, of this particular combination. He treats the chord on its own merits

ELGAR (*The Apostles*).

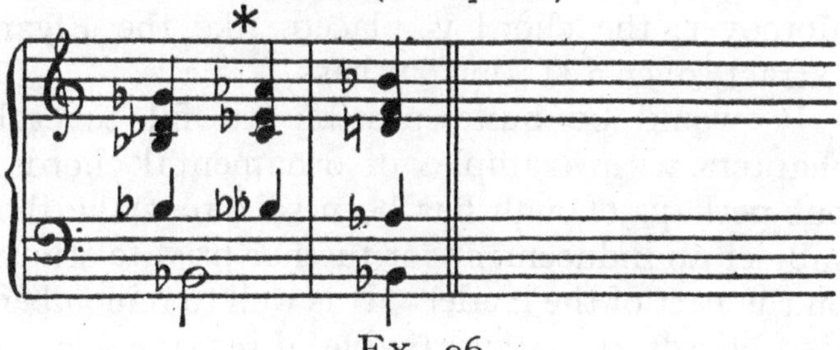

Ex. 96

as a chord, and follows it with a most beautiful and perfectly natural resolution. Sir Edward Elgar uses the chord, over a sustained bass, in much the same way, i.e. by treating it as an accepted combination of sound in itself requiring no apology or explanation (Ex. 96).

We may regard the A flat as a satellite of G flat, which it displaces. The extract is also an example of a passing chord, proceeding by easily followed melodic steps, joining two other comparatively simple chords. Further varieties of the chord are shown in Ex. 97.

At A, the D natural is treated as an appoggiatura resolving on to C, which it temporally displaces; at B, there is a similar treatment over an ornamental bass, the whole combination having the sound of a borrowed chord, viz. that known as a dominant thirteenth of C flat; at C there are no less than three satellites: (1) D natural displacing C, and E sharp and G sharp displacing F sharp and A respectively. Moreover, the chord is placed, like the Elgar extract, over a stationary bass.

It would be quite possible to fill several chapters with examples of ornamental chords, but perhaps enough has been said to make the subject an inducement for further private study on the part of the reader. It is well to remember that chords are often capable of many explanations, and while it is useful and instructive to examine every possible explanation, it is wise to accept the simplest if it is adequate.

SULLIVAN (*Who is like unto Thee?*).

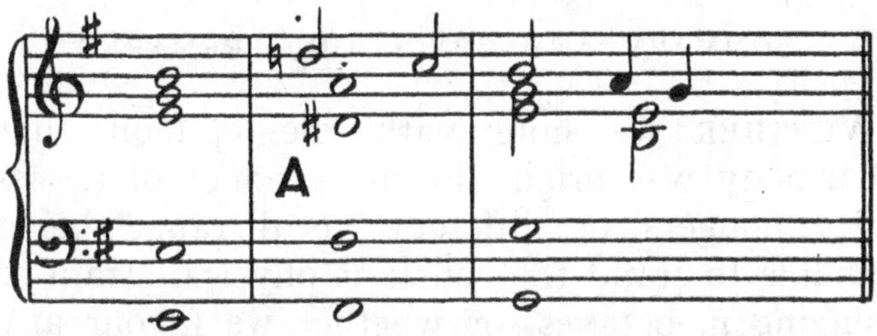

C. MACPHERSON (*In the Lord put I my trust*).

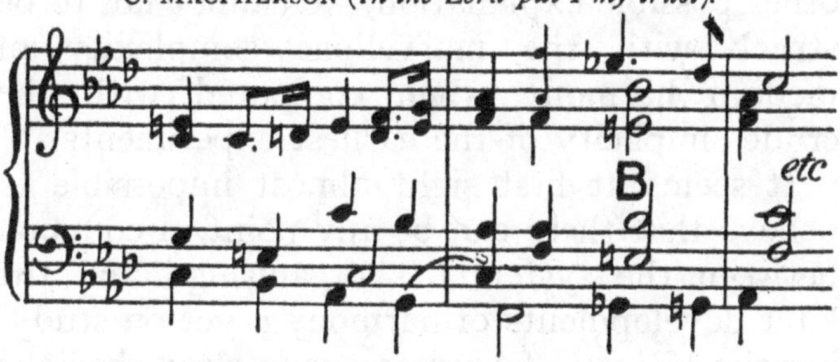

ALAN GRAY (Idyll No. 6, *Recessional*—for organ).

Ex. 97

CHAPTER VIII

SUMMARY AND CONCLUDING REMARKS

WHETHER we hold with the opinion that harmony was originally the product of necessity, singers of different vocal range being unable to stand the constant physical strain of singing in octaves, or whether we favour any other possible explanation, we cannot fail to be struck with the marvellous complexity of modern harmony when compared with the crude simplicity of the earliest experiments.

It seems at first sight almost impossible to believe that there can be any point in common between the system of 'organising' and the later developments of harmony; yet on studying the history of harmony it is clear that the whole process of its unfolding has been both obvious and logical.

It is, however, most important to remember that the difficult stages in the progress of harmony do not imply that old methods were suddenly discarded while new ones were universally adopted. As in our own day there are certain musicians who write in a style peculiar to themselves, and also those who employ older-established forms of harmonic-idiom, so in the past there was the same overlapping of methods, some composers adopting the new while others retained the old style.

The process has been rather like the effect of 'dissolving views,' in which the impression of the first picture grows fainter as the succeeding one increases in definition. The simile has one drawback, however, as the two pictures might have nothing in common—a picture of a battleship might melt into one of a flower-garden—but excepting that rather unfortunate difference the simile holds good.

Any plan of showing the developments of harmony in the form of a short table is somewhat in the nature of an experiment, and the following, though perhaps sequentially correct, is by no means exhaustive; nor is it entirely explanatory on account of the many overlappings of systems to which we have referred.

I. '*Organising,*' *discant,* and *faux-bourdons,* in due course merging into

II. disciplined *counterpoint,* in which were used—

(*a*) passing and other discordant ornamental notes *off* the accent and

(*b*) suspensions *on* the accent.

III. Chords produced by II (*a*) in process of time were used *on* the accent, and later still were employed without being 'prepared'; the latter remark applies to the combinations produced by II (*b*).

IV. Free use of the *appoggiatura* and kindred ornaments, causing temporary derangement of chords.

V. Growth of *chromatics* making further alterations of chords, and tending to add an element of mystery and uncertainty as to key-centres.

VI. The æsthetic application of *acoustics*, suggesting experiments in harmony and providing fancy scales, novel cadences, and such like.

In reading the above table we must not forget that ancient harmony was regarded from the contrapuntal standpoint, whereas from the time of Bach counterpoint has been approached largely from the harmonic point of view. The harmonic basis of observation has become so enlarged and experimentally involved, that there is a present danger of the contrapuntal aspect being overlooked.

We have in the early chapters attempted to show that nearly the whole of the older harmonic progress was the result of vertical slices of unaccented counterpoint being transferred to the accent, such as:

Ex. 98

and it is not too much to claim for this system of 'transplanting' that it has been perhaps more prolific than any other in producing new chords, and also that its possibilities are far from being exhausted.

We will make a few brief remarks on the last two headings of the table (V and VI). The free use of chromatics in composition naturally caused at first great discussion. The old contrapuntal writers were just as much, if not more, disturbed, when Monteverde introduced unprepared discords; and while it may be justly claimed that the chromatic alteration of a chord makes all the difference, it is questionable whether the difference is so great as that between a discord on the accent and a discord off the accent.

There is little doubt that the great sustaining

power of the modern pianoforte acts as a direct stimulus to composers in finding out new effects in harmony; it is perhaps partly responsible for the partial neglect of counterpoint when the present era is compared with former times.

It may be true that the desire for harmonic experiment increases in proportion with the sustaining power of the instrument; it certainly is true that many modern 'atmospheric' compositions cannot be rendered properly on a piano of poor sustaining power. Those who have had the pleasure of playing harpsichords and other forerunners of the piano will have noticed at once how well suited to the character of these instruments is the music which was written for them. The short, dry, and spiky little twanging notes of a harpsichord were well suited to rapidly-moving contrapuntal music, while they were entirely unsuited to music of a purely melodic nature. It was usual in music of the latter type to deck the melodic portion with all sorts of ornaments in order to draw attention to the melody, a device wholly due to the lack of the sustaining power of the instruments. As soon as the skill of piano makers supplied this latter deficiency a new field was open to composers; they were not slow to take advantage of the mechanical improvements, the effects of which were firstly noticeable in melody, and secondly in harmonic enterprise.

The connection between artistic device and mechanical means of expression forms a subject large enough to fill a volume. There is one aspect of the matter to which the writer has made reference when lecturing. Seeing how much Bach and Purcell accomplished for harmony in the way of inventing new combinations, it sometimes appears remarkable that few new harmonic combinations were added by such a giant as Beethoven, and other composers of his time, with the possible chief exception of Schubert. The writer has ventured the opinion that, having to think in terms suited to such instruments as the valveless trumpet and natural horn, which only sounded the harmonics of the foundation note (p. 13), composers who constantly employed these instruments began to write all their music within certain prescribed harmonic limits. Though we may never hear more beautiful horn effects than some which Beethoven wrote, there is no doubt that the introduction of horns and trumpets with valves, which enabled players to produce any note, effected an enormous influence upon composition generally, and harmony in particular.

Regarding the last heading of the table (VI)

it is as well to state that the whole question of matters relating to the practical connection between acoustics and composition is as yet open to discussion. That the harmonic vocabulary has been enormously increased by what one cannot entirely dissociate from scientific methods, seems beyond doubt ; but these are yet early days to say how much of this vocabulary will pass into the accepted language of music. It must not be thought that the employment of harmonics and summational tones necessarily makes new chords. These fancy notes are sounded as the suggestions of some usually fairly simple chord. They really reinforce notes which are dimly already there. This statement is merely explanatory, and neither condemns nor justifies the modern use of these notes.

When we refer to a work as being harmonically 'modern,' we should always be careful to remember that the term connotes neither badness nor goodness. These characteristics are found in the works of every age. The only thing that counts in any composition, is, the guiding inspiration of the composer. *How* he says a thing is undoubtedly of great importance, but *what* he says is more important.

In this age of numberless harmonic idioms people are sometimes carried away by a composer who says nothing in a most effective manner. A string of new harmonic effects will often induce the hearer to place too high a value on some composition; while perhaps another piece of music of greater worth but with less harmonic ambition will be rated dull. In forming our opinion as to the merits of any new and difficult work we should, certainly as far as harmony is concerned, be guided by what has happened in the past.

In an early chapter we saw how the wild experiments in performing two or more tunes simultaneously eventually settled down into the staid practice of counterpoint. There is a modern counterpart of this where composers have used different progressions of harmonies each pursuing an independent logical course without reference to vertical suitability. As discant, when robbed of its vertical impossibilities, grew into counterpoint, so perhaps textbooks in the far future will give instructions on how to write counterpoint with strands of harmony in the place of single melodies. This is a far-fetched improbability though not an actual impossibility, and it is mentioned only for the purpose of showing how important it is to keep an open mind in dealing with matters yet in the making.

What is considered ugly now may be thought

beautiful in time to come. Many accepted effects in harmony were long considered ugly because they were not understood; the connection between them and their prototypes was not grasped at once.

What is beauty to a long-sighted few, and is still ugliness to the majority, naturally cannot be classed among accepted effects; it is only when disputed abnormalities have become more or less commonplaces that their true artistic value can be rightly judged. For this reason inventors in the world of harmony receive little encouragement or general appreciation at first, but it is safe to say that their efforts will meet with the recognition or rejection they deserve, in proportion as they have been prompted by the combined and balanced effort of both head and heart. Works which are entirely the result of head-work will in due course, like works in other spheres of art, take their place among those which make little or no human appeal. So too, works which are entirely the products of the heart and have little or no intellectual bias, will find their due level in perhaps appealing only to those whose feelings are not regulated by any intellectual impulse.

Harmony, whether as a science or as the outcome of purely æsthetic motives, can never stand still. As in times gone by there have been great changes wrought in the practice of harmony by the introduction of new mechanical means of expression, so we may expect that the future will see developments of which we probably have no idea at present.

Before instrumental music was established, harmony was of a simple kind entirely suited to the vocal efforts of performers. The gradual employment of various instruments, untrammelled by vocal limitations, familiarised strange new chords which were in turn transferred to vocal music ; the result is that singers are now called upon to perform passages which would have been considered impossible in a former age. Here we see a reversal of things, for in early days it was vocal music that gave the idiom to instrumental music ; now it is instrumental music that influences vocal technique, both in melody and harmony.

It is idle to prophesy, but perhaps the day will come again when vocal attainment will exceed instrumental and point the way to novel harmonic effects. Perhaps singers will divide the scale into smaller degrees than a semitone, though the present attitude towards those who unwillingly accomplish this feat is not encouraging.

There is one matter about harmony, or more particularly, progressions, which has received little attention in this work. The methods of composers have been mentioned, but only one of them, namely, the whole-tone scale, has received any degree of analysis.

We have stated in an earlier chapter that single chords are of no value by themselves, there must be two or more chords to define a key, i.e. there must be some progression. Now, a great many of the harmonic characteristics of certain composers are less evident in the chords that are used than in the manner of following these with other chords. That implies that though a single chord may be interesting as an unit of sound, its value depends upon its progress to another chord.

Progressions therefore betray more character than single chords. Modern harmony teems with instances where some plan has been adopted, quite possibly from æsthetic motives only. We can but hint at a few of the simpler devices in addition to those already described at fuller length.

The practice of using—

(1) progressions of triads and other chords which have some note in common :

(2) any chord, preferably a discord, and moving it about by tones or semitones regardless of the ordinary rules of part-writing :

(3) a scale of any description, chromatic for choice, in any voice or part, as a suggestive framework on which to build harmony :

(4) progressions in contrary motion designed to meet at a certain point, a process often demanding harmonic invention at awkward corners :

(5) discords of the appoggiatura description, and quitting them without their normal resolution :

(6) some preconceived pattern of motion to which the progressions are forced to adapt themselves.

These form but a few of numberless designs or systems all of which have helped to extend the outlook of harmony.

Some of the methods named are obviously of greater artistic value than others ; perhaps none require less inventive faculty than the second, which is included merely to give a fairly typical selection.

Some musicians who do not compose music often ask, 'What is the use of learning harmony?' The answer is that, whether they are pianists or singers, the study of harmony will enable them to become good readers at sight. This is a qualification which cannot be valued too highly, or the lack of it condemned too strongly. A knowledge of harmony enables a pianist to analyse at sight the chord he has to play, while it helps a singer to know his proper note in a chord if he has not the gift of absolute pitch. To the composer a systematic course of harmony is indispensable, and no apology is needed in enforcing this obvious fact.

Whether those to whom music is essentially a pastime think that harmony is worthy of further attention or not, the author cannot say. He can only hope they do.

In conclusion, we urge the importance of keeping an open mind with regard to new harmonic effects. If strange chords or progressions do not please us at once, it is unwise to put them aside without further consideration : we should rather ask ourselves whether we understand them or not. If not, then we have no right to condemn them even though we dislike them. Of course it is always easier to say 'I don't like' than 'I don't understand,' but the latter is usually the fairer attitude towards novelties of any description.

An account of a recent concert reported in *The Times* affords an illuminating commentary on the foregoing remarks. The concert was given by a composer well known for his original harmonies. The writer of the report said: "... It made two things clear. First, it proved once more how little there is of music that notation can express, or at any rate that in some music the best part is left unexpressed. Next"—this is the important point—"that when the composer can play—and there was no doubt about that last night—he can show us things which we could not have guessed for ourselves. Mr. —— made us understand, just as Ravel did a couple of years ago, that what appear crudities on paper are just the natural way you would express yourself if you had it in you. . . ."

If it is not in you, do not be too harsh in expressing your opinion. However much some people may dislike anything new in harmony, they should realise that judging by the past there is sure to be further advance. They cannot prevent it. If they think they can (though some progress may be experimental and unsuccessful) they place themselves much in the same dangerous position as those daring small boys who delight to hang on to the backs of carts drawn by strong horses and slide along the streets. It is very bad for their boots.

The author often wonders whether it is right to say that the process of harmonic development has been marked by alternate phases which may be termed 'solid' and 'fluid.' The earliest and most rigid 'organising' was a solid, because only one form of harmony was used for each note. The second form of organising with its greater variety of intervals was thus more in the nature of a fluid. Then came discant, an undoubted solid, for all the voices proceeded under hard and fast rules, viz. that the tune allotted to each voice was to be performed regardless of vertical effect. In turn this practice under the melting influence of disciplined counterpoint became a fluid. A 'solid' period arrived again when the unaccented discords of counterpoint were transferred to the accents and subjected to fixed resolutions. The fiery experiments of later harmony have treated most of these discords in such a manner as to render them likely to become fluid again.

The still newer methods, embracing such things as new scales and the like (often with a strong backing of a quasi-scientific element) are bringing about the return to a solid phase. It remains a question which of the two conditions has produced the greatest results. A vote would more than likely turn largely in favour of the fluid condition.

These two conditions 'solid' and 'fluid,'

both regarding form and harmony, probably constitute the two poles between which may be found most of the subjects of controversy connected with the general aspect towards music.

THE END

ALPHABETICAL LIST OF COMPOSERS OF EXAMPLES

	Number of Examples.
Adam de la Hale	11
Bach, J. S.	17, 18, 47, 48, 49, 74
Beethoven	19, 55, 57, 62
Creyghton	34, 35, 36
Dale, B.	75, 80
Dufay	28
Elgar, Sir E.	96
Gray, Alan	97
Haydn	67
Hucbald	9
Josquin de Prés	30
King, Charles	37
Landino	26
Macpherson, C.	97
Mendelssohn	5
Monteverde	33
Palestrina	31,32
Purcell	43, 44, 45, 46
Rachmaninoff	6
Ravel	87, 88
Schumann	69
Stradella	42
Strauss, R.	77, 79
Sullivan	97
Wagner	64
Weber	59
Wesley, S. S.	47*a*

INDEX